Fearless Connection

REAL LIFE STORIES OF ENTREPRENEURS
WHO MADE IT HAPPEN!

NICOLA PEAKE

I dedicate this book to the incredible people that have supported me on my journey so far. To my amazing family, my friends and mentors and of course all of my incredible Peakes members who have supported me on my Peakes journey.

There have been times which have been challenging, and of course lots of fun and lovely experiences with you all! Thank you for being with me.

ACKNOWLEDGEMENTS

Writing a book like this takes effort and there are lots of people that made this happen! Firstly to my amazing authors, thank you for being brave and getting your message out there!

To the amazing Charlie Brown, thank you for your lovely images and a really fun photo shoot.

Thanks to the team at Discover Your Bounce Publishing and Mark from Brand 51 for the cool cover.

And finally thanks to you, for buying this book!

CONTENTS

FOREWORD
By Leona Burton

In today's fast-paced business world, success is often determined by not only what you know but who you know. Building connections and networks is essential for achieving business success, and this collaboration book is a valuable resource for anyone seeking to enhance their network and build meaningful relationships.

The authors of this book have joined forces to provide insights, strategies, and practical tips on how to build and nurture connections that can lead to business success. Each author brings a unique perspective, expertise, and experience that add value for you, the reader.

Whether you are an entrepreneur, a business professional, or a career-minded individual, this book will provide you with actionable insights on how to build connections that can help you achieve your goals. From networking events to social media platforms, the authors discuss a range of strategies and tactics that can help you expand your reach and build valuable relationships.

The stories shared in this book are proof that building connections and networks is not only necessary but also rewarding. By following the advice of the authors, you can learn how to leverage your connections and create opportunities for yourself and others.

I highly recommend this book to anyone who wants to enhance their networking skills and achieve greater success in business. It's a must-read for anyone who wants to learn how to build meaningful connections that can lead to lifelong relationships and success.

Leona Burton, MIB International

INTRODUCTION

When I started Peakes Private Members Club my drive was to bring together ambitious business owners, to give them the community that I missed when running my first business. I wanted to create a welcoming network which would provide a sense of belonging, as well as a place online and offline where people could create real connections. It would be a place for us to share our good days – and our bad ones without any fear of judgement or cliques!

I knew my events had to be unique and different. I wanted them to be fun, inclusive, not just sales pitches and suits! I wanted to create a great atmosphere where people would feel comfortable, and where they could support each other, learn from each other and have a giggle.

The idea for this book came when I realised just how much knowledge we have between us. With more people than ever deciding to start their own business, the skills we have gathered and the stories of our challenges and triumphs will really help you to navigate the bumps in the road that can arise.

If you are reading this book, use it as your 'go to' guide, when maybe you are having a tricky day, or trying to scale and grow.

Nicola Peake

NICOLA PEAKE

Nicola grew up as an only child in a council house in Birmingham. She didn't really enjoy school, and as soon as she could work she found herself a waitressing job. She left school at 16, as the fun and excitement of working with new people was a much better option to her than having to do her A Levels!

At 17, she decided to look for a new job, and she landed a job in a bank, even after an awful Maths grade at GCSE. By 20, Nicola was a young mom, progressing into new roles within the bank. She was stubborn, ambitious and wanted to succeed, even when people didn't think she could, so she studied and within a few years, she was a qualified financial adviser.

Nicola loved her work, she met so many incredible people, from her colleagues to her clients. However, after spending over 20 years building her career, it all crashed down around her, and after a year of hell Nicola decided to give up the career she had worked so hard to build to pursue happiness instead.

She took a huge risk to create her own new business with no experience, no money and no idea on what to do or where to start. Nicola grew this business to six figures within 12 months, before selling it. Although she loved the business and it was a huge success, she missed spending time with others, and working alone every day led her to not enjoy running the business she'd lovingly built. She decided that she had risked everything once, and of course she could do it again, so she created and launched her second business. This was created through her passion to work with people again, and to help connect other business owners who also wanted to be around people. Peakes Private Members Club was opened in December 2021, and this is now a successful networking business with over 100 incredible business owners. Without this business, she would not have so many amazing people in her life and this book would not be here.

Find out more at www.linktr.ee/nicolapeake

Embracing Risk for Success

January 2021, we were all back into lockdown. I was six months into running my new business and it was going better than I could ever have imagined.

I was delivering afternoon teas all over the UK. What started as an idea whilst drinking wine in the garden, right at the start of lockdown, was now a fully-fledged business, quickly going from £1,000 months to £20,000 months, and the best bit at the time was I could do it all from home.

I loved it. I was in amazing publications – my business was even listed next to Rick Stein as one of the top food delivery businesses! I received amazing reviews, and my diary was fully booked. At this time, my daughter and husband were at home, places were closed, and no one was out and about.

I made a lot of new friends online during lockdown. Most days, I would be online before and after the kitchen chaos! I would join Clubhouse chats and Zoom calls, packing boxes whilst building relationships! Voice notes suddenly became the best way for me to communicate and I had some great fun and laughs during this time with people I was meeting. You know who you are!

By July, the world was slowly getting back to normal. The pubs and restaurants were back open, and people were starting to go out. My orders now included events, such as christenings, birthdays, and weddings, as well as the daily deliveries I had to prepare. I was working six, sometimes seven days a week – I never worked weekends when I was employed, and it wasn't something I wanted to do. I was stuck in my kitchen every single day, alone. I started to resent my own business. My life before this was sociable. My job meant I worked with people every single day. I visited my clients every day. I was rarely alone, and I loved it. I love people, connection, and building new relationships, and the business I had lovingly created had none of this.

I could have gone networking, and I did think about it. I decided I would start to block out a day a week to get back out there and meet new people. The experiences I had networking were pretty awful. You know the ones, 6am starts, dry bacon roll, pinstripe suits, and those horrid 60-second pitches of shame! Did I really want to start doing this again? NO!

I looked around for different types of events. Ones where I would meet people like me, those who ran businesses; and although they wanted to 'network', they also just wanted some time out of their working day to meet new people, build relationships, and get to know people better.

I didn't find it, so suddenly all my thoughts turned to something new.

I decided it was time to take on another new venture!

Make the change

Today I am known for my new business, which is an inclusive networking community, Peakes Private Members Club, or 'Peakes' for short!

Over the last two years I have learnt a lot about setting up businesses. I have made mistakes, felt overwhelmed, and become frustrated when things weren't moving as fast as I wanted them too. However, it has all been worth it, and I want to make sure that you learn something from me and all the other amazing authors in this book.

This isn't just another book of life stories. Rags to riches, trauma to success, in debt to making millions. As inspirational as they can be, let's be honest, sometimes they can be a bit boring, done to death, with no real tangible outcomes you can take hold of and use.

I want you to learn from us, I want you to feel you can take action, even if it's imperfect, and I want you to enjoy your own success, however that looks for you.

I will start by telling you a bit about me. I am an only child. I lived with my mom and although I had a loving home, I did get lonely and bored. I would receive games like Hungry Hippos and Monopoly for birthdays and Christmases, but I wouldn't have anyone to play them with.

Growing up, I always wanted to be out with friends. I would be calling them at 8am on Saturdays, no doubt annoying them when they just wanted to sleep and I wanted to be out, enjoying the company.

I left school at 16, I didn't go to college or university. I never felt clever enough, and I just wanted to work and earn money. I worked as a waitress at a huge hotel, and I loved it! I made loads of friends and had a great social life (the days before mortgages, rent and bills)! At 17 years old, I decided I needed to try and find a proper job, and went to work for a high street bank.

I worked with so many people, some are still my closest friends to this day. I thrived by being around people, whether that was friends, colleagues or clients, it's what made me tick.

I was always good at talking! I was called a chatterbox in my school reports, I guess I liked the sound of my own voice. It's not like I had to fight to be heard as a child, as it was only me! This trait, which was always perceived to be a bad thing at school, led me to build a great career, building relationships, by being able to talk to anyone.

Joining the bank paved the way for my whole career. By my early 20s I was a fully qualified financial adviser with a beautiful daughter. There weren't many females doing this at that time, especially so young. There was so much misogyny, sleazy managers, and underhand comments. I used to have my name listed on league tables which were faxed to every branch in the Midlands with 'The Single Mum' is at the top again. This was so wrong, but just accepted back then. However, there were so many good times. We had brilliant nights out, fun days at work, pub lunches, Christmas parties, booze bus tours, and there was always someone who had your back.

I went on to work with everyone from farmers to business owners; I was employed and self-employed; and I enjoyed luxury incentives and holidays – it was a great career.

I worked doing what I loved until I was 41. I had hundreds of clients over the years. My days were filled visiting my clients' homes or working alongside others. If I was driving about, I would be on calls to friends, clients, colleagues. My life was full of people.

So, you see, although I had this amazing new business in 2021 which I was so proud of, I had lost all of this. I was suddenly alone, and although I had made lots of new connections online, I knew I needed more.

I didn't want to go back into the corporate world, so I had to create something myself. A business which I wouldn't end up resenting, a business full of people, one which would bring me joy and joy to others. So, I did.

It can be hard to accept that something you have worked so hard to build is no longer your passion. When I first started to feel apathy for my business, I tried to bury it. I was so scared to admit it to myself, and I kept going for months. An order would come through and I would roll my eyes, people would enquire for events and I would either say I was fully booked or quote a significant price. All those excited feelings, the butterflies, the sheer delight at receiving orders had gone.

Have you felt like this? Whether you have your own business or you're employed, do you find that you also dread new enquiries, new business or having to deliver on something you've sold?

If the answer is yes, it is time to really look at what is making you feel unhappy doing what you are doing. Sometimes, it could just mean you need a rest, you could be near burnout, and your mind may not be in the right place. But, if you know deep down it is because you are doing something that you no longer love, then what can you do to *make the change*?

I had to sit and reflect on what I love doing. What could I bring into my business that I would never be bored of?

This started with my personal loves:

- I love being around people;

- I love to do nice things, go to nice bars, restaurants, events. Ultimately, socialising:

- I love getting to know people on a deeper level; and

- I love bringing people together.

There are a good few of my closest friends who met through me (I am the person who invites every man and his dog on a night out).

It made sense to me to try and build a community of other business owners who were the same.

There had to be more people like me who didn't like the sleazy networking meetings. I thought to myself, surely there must be other people who are happy to just take a day out of their business to meet for lunch and chat about anything for a few hours. There must be others out there missing real connections. There must be people who want to make business friends and enjoy doing nice things together, and all of these brilliant people I've met online, surely, they want to meet in real life too?

And yes, there were, and I found them. I don't just have a great business now, I have a great lifestyle, and a whole load of amazing new friends.

My advice to you when you are ready is to *make the change*.

Invest in yourself and your learning

There will inevitably be things in business that you do not know, especially when you are starting from scratch and have never done anything like this before. So, it's only logical that you will need to invest both time and money into yourself and your business. Being able to learn from mentors and coaches who have the experience to make suggestions about how you could grow your business, and support you in doing so, is invaluable.

I have found that working 1-1 with a mentor helps to push me, hold me accountable and 'kick my ass' when needed! Working within a mastermind or group setting helps to inspire and empower me. Receiving support from my peers, helping one another to realise our goals, and seeing the potential in one another, is priceless.

This will naturally mean that initially, your profits won't be as high, as your turnover will be reinvested. But it does mean that when investing in the right areas, your business will grow at a far faster rate than if you didn't invest. The profit will come, and there will be more of it, but you do need patience before just drawing the profits for personal pleasure.

In December 2022, I invested £1000 to spend two hours with a marketing mentor. Now, I may not have done this in the very early days, but the clarity, advice, and accountability it gave me led me to generate £40,000 in sales a week later. So, it was really worth the investment!

When investing, try to think long term. How will investing your time and money now help you in the future? Not chasing after every shiny thing that's laid in front of you, because believe me, you will be inundated with offers to help make your business £8million in eight hours! But, by asking yourself how you can grow and scale your business so you can decide which areas you need support with and then investing accordingly.

Take action

Imposter syndrome can play a huge role in our lives, whether personally or in business. The voice inside that tells us we 'aren't ready', 'aren't good enough', that we need more experience and so on. It's there, within our subconscious, to keep us safe from potential threats. The trouble is, though, anything that is new is perceived as a 'threat'. So, when you start a new business, when you bring out a new offering in said business, when you try

14

a new strategy or make a pivot, it's there.

In business, you need to push yourself. It will feel terrifying at times to take that step out of your comfort zone, but that's the only way you are going to reach your goals. Taking action is key to the success of your business. If you sit there, without taking action, you are effectively 'leaving money on the table'.

I've always found that when you know you need to do something in business that scares you and makes you want to run in the opposite direction, the best thing you can do is face it head-on, there and then. Pushing it to one side (and, no doubt, trying to pretend it isn't there!) will likely lead to procrastination. The longer you leave it, the harder it will seem.

Take action in your business. Now. Taking fast action within my businesses led to fast results, and it can for you, too.

The thing we often don't realise when setting up a business is that things not going to plan or 'making a mistake' is just as valuable as something going right. It may not have led to the outcome you were hoping for, but it can be used as a useful tool to assess how to do things better the next time around. So, try not to let a fear of failure hold you back – the only true failure would be not ever trying to make a success of your business.

It's easy to ask ourselves, "But what if we fail?" In the famous words of Erin Hanson, "Oh but my darling, what if you fly?"

Build genuine connections

If you only want a customer to buy from you once, cold-selling will no doubt work. In the majority of cases though, the only way you are going to get those long-term, loyal clients that keep returning to buy from you is through the relationship you build with them.

I'm not talking fake, surface-layer relationships. I mean building genuine connections with the *right* clients for you.

At the start of your business, it can be so exciting to see clients coming through your metaphorical door that you will welcome anyone. But once you start to niche and work out exactly who your ideal client is, you will be able to target them in your messaging and seek them out.

Working with the right people can help ignite that fire in your belly. In order to attract these people, you need to let them know why you'd like to connect with them, and how you can help them. Help to support them, even if it's something as simple as interacting with their social media posts, and they will likely offer you the same in return.

Allowing yourself to be open to meeting new people is key. Get to know them, listen to them, take an interest in what they have to say. Just as you would build a friendship in the 'real world', build friendships and connections in the business world too. Even if someone isn't your 'ideal client', they may know someone who is.

Word of mouth is invaluable when welcoming new clients. Having someone 'vouch' for you can be the difference between making the sale or not. The larger your circle or network, the larger your potential market.

If I hadn't expanded my circle and worked on building relationships as much as I could, I wouldn't now have over 100 amazing business owners in my community a year after launching.

YOU get to decide today whether you are going to make a success of your business, and whether you're going to do that quickly. Everyone's version of 'success' is unique to them, and we all have different goals, but how would you like your business to look a year from today? Now ask yourself, how will you invest in yourself to get there? What action will you take? What connections will you build?

It's possible for you to grow your business, with no experience, to six figures (or more!) within 12 months. I'm living proof of that. Now is your time to create your story of success.

What is my long-term vision?

I'm not going to lie; I want to earn a lot of money. I want the financial freedom I have always craved. That doesn't necessarily mean I want lots of money to buy a big car, house, holiday or designer goods, although I wouldn't say no! Freedom to me is to have no debts, to be able to do impulsive things like nights out, weekend breaks, treat my family, and to keep investing in myself and my business. I want to be in a position where I don't need to check my bank balance before a shopping trip or holiday.

I want to bring 250 members into Peakes and help create thousands of amazing new connections. I want my own network to grow, and I want to take every opportunity I can to build my own business, profile, and connections.

I want to inspire and help hundreds of people to follow their passion and their dreams. Life is too short to be in an unhappy workplace, or to be working all hours running a business you resent. You deserve to be happy, for you and for everyone around you. So, let me ask you, what can you do now to **make the change** and make your life happier?

I would love to help you on your own business journey. Throughout this book you are going to be given so much valuable advice from these incredible people who I have built relationships with, if you are ready to take action, create new connections and receive the support you need, come and join us in Peakes Private Members Club.

AMANDA FAYE

Amanda Faye is a proud mother of five beautiful and talented children and a grandmother to a gorgeous grandbaby. She is the founder and owner of Childcare Solution LTD, founded in 2006. CCS was set up to provide children and families with out of school care within the local community. Over the years they have set up five sites across the borough serving over 500 families over their 17 years of service. They have also started a leadership programme for young people in year 11 to give them knowledge and experience to build on their confidence and presence in the workplace. Over the next three years Amanda hopes to extend their provision to cater for early years, caring for babies and toddlers. She would also like to deliver programmes and workshops that will help to support and strengthen families raising children in such challenging times.

Amanda is totally addicted to training and exercising as she is able switch off and be in the moment. Zumba is her go to class as she loves the social side of being around like-minded people. It keeps her sane and helps her to manage all that she does.

Find out more about Amanda at www.linktr.ee/amanda_faye

The Unfolding Of Your Purpose

It's amazing to think the little girl who was frequently called into the head teacher's office to have informal discussions on school activity and playground gossip, would go on to run a childcare organisation of her own. She often imagined herself sitting on the other side of the head teacher's desk, with her legs crossed and hands clasped together; as he did. Unknown to her, she was a natural born leader and someone that was set apart from her peers. She would take a stand for others, as identified in the early stages of her life. In secondary school, she went on to become the chair of the school council. Her objective was to be a representative for the diverse groups and individuals in the school, to be fair and inclusive, to impact school life and offer practical solutions for positive change and outcomes.

No prizes for guessing that little girl was me!

Over the years, I have come to realise that I have always had a calling to serve, to be a mother to many and to be the matriarch in my family.

Becoming a mother of five children has most certainly been my greatest teacher. It has taught me love like I've never known. An unconditional love that gives from deep within, a love that seeks to know and understand and to make me a better version of myself.

My serving extended beyond my family to my wider community, providing a safe and stimulating environment for children to grow, be nurtured and develop. A space where families felt, and knew, they were part of our extended family.

In 2006, I set up an out of school provision, providing breakfast, after-school and holiday clubs for children and families within our local community. It was created to give parents peace of mind while working or studying, allowing their children and young people to take ownership of their play environment and development. It was an environment they could call their own, make friends, play, be themselves, celebrate themselves and each other, learn new skills and build their confidence and self-esteem.

Looking back, I had to overcome many hurdles to see the business through. The idea, the vision and the mission statement were all written based on my personal standards and requirements as a parent. The policies, procedures, handbooks and programmes were a culmination of present and existing documentation already provided by local authority and Ofsted guidelines. These were meticulously studied, dissected and recreated, all ready to be implemented. Securing premises was our greatest challenge. Not that I needed to approach many different properties, I knew where it needed to be. The location itself was essential for proximity to local schools, the challenge came with the bureaucracy.

I attended a meeting where I had to deliver a presentation to the church hall committee, who had the responsibility to decide if they would offer us a rental agreement to hire the church hall. After agreeing and supporting the idea and vison, they moved the goal posts. I was called back to attend another meeting with a second hall committee, and on more than one occasion they posed additional conditions which needed to be met. This went on for some time, delaying our opening and delivery of service. We'd take two steps forward and five steps back. I answered every question asked and provided evidence to dispel all uncertainties. I ensured the rules and requirements were followed and met, and knew my heart was in the right place. I was offering who I was, what I stood for and believed; all that I had learnt over my years as an early years' practitioner, as a mother, but more importantly, as a someone walking in their purpose.

It all began at a place I loved working – Springfield – a stone's throw from where I lived and the area I knew. The centre was part of the wider community and adopted the spirit surrounding it. The after-school club had formed its own committee which was called 'The Friends of Springfield', and that they certainly were. The committee was a collective of parents, staff and local residents who were all embraced as members of the community. The staff did an amazing job at welcoming and connecting with all who entered the doors of the centre.

Many community events took place: family discos, barbeques, Bingo, bring and buy sales and family trips to the seaside. This was the foundation of what I would then go on to further develop. An extended family where each person felt valued and significant. Everyone had a part to play, and everyone's role was just as important as everyone else's. I learnt about community spirit and commitment. I reaffirmed my understanding of serving and giving for a greater cause and purpose.

This was a local authority-run project, one where fundraising was a necessity, and the community came together to maintain its social purpose. I established great relationships and built strong rapport with both staff and families. My ability to connect with people and my positive work ethic did not go unnoticed. I was keen to put myself forward, to give ideas and suggestions, to offer additional support, to take the lead by using my initiative and being a positive individual that others enjoyed being around. I proved to be a reliable individual who quite quickly became a significant team and community member.

I was approached by a Project Manager in Hackney, who was considering several after-school settings in a cluster of schools in the borough, to manage one of the sites. Completely taken back and overwhelmed, I acknowledged that Springfield had given me the platform to showcase my leadership skills and passion for children and families.

Through my journey, I have clearly seen the mapping of each stage of my life and the individual steps that moved me forward on my path to setting up and running my own business. Being confident in my abilities and not shying away from my innate gifts and purpose has certainly brought me a long way.

So often we try to blend into our environment. We try to avoid drawing attention to ourselves, to not offend or disrupt the status quo, not realising that each of us has a unique gift to offer the world. Our place cannot be filled by any other when we give of ourselves authentically – we will shine. And for most people who cross our paths, our light will make them feel loved and inspired. They will gravitate to us and receive all the good things we offer to them, helping to take them to a higher level of existence.

Based in a Hackney school, I managed two members of staff and was responsible for 30 children. My passion drove every aspect of the club. Guidelines were provided by The Learning Trust, but we developed our own planning structure that was strictly based on our children's interests. It included drama, dance, woodwork, sports, sewing, construction etc. We never settled for the basic standard; in our eyes every child mattered, and it was in our interest to see to it that they knew they mattered. Every personality and every ability were taken into consideration. I would prepare resources for the children at home. Additional resources were sought from local sources and our children got to experience a play environment that allowed them to explore and experiment.

We soon became a flagship site within The Learning Trust after-school clubs. We were visited by the Hackney Guardian newspaper who featured our talent show in their weekly issue. I worked in close partnership with our parents and the school we serviced. I held regular meetings with the school's head teacher to keep her updated with our plans and programmes of activities, and to keep her informed of the children's developments and concerns, if any came up. The head would also share relevant information that helped us to better support the children in our care.

I was asked to lead a manager's meeting to share good practice from our setting with our senior practitioners. Being asked to lead as an example of excellence highlighted that we were serving our children and families with a high standard of service, and it was evident that others were being challenged to raise their standard. A few managers celebrated our achievements, others didn't appreciate the pressure our success was putting on them and saw it as an additional load and burden. Your mindset determines how you view the world around you, is your cup half full or half empty? It would be nice to believe that examples of good practice offer inspiration and direction. It should motivate others to strive for better, for themselves and others. In this respect we determine our own destiny. Why put a ceiling on our capabilities and possibilities when we could be reaching for the sky?

Passion drives you, but purpose leads you. When you become tired and weary on the journey, your purpose sustains you, along with the support of a good team. Surrounding yourself with the right people is essential when people can pour into you as you have poured into them. It keeps you moving and helps you evolve. When you walk in your purpose you are rewarded by impact and positive change. Although validation is something human beings naturally seek; our validation comes in the form of seeing a difference in the lives of others, be it one or many.

My line manager identified my efforts as special, and although the borough and children within my setting benefitted from my efforts, I was identified as having potential to run my own enterprise outside of the council. I was put forward for a level three qualification in Child Development and Playwork, as this was the basic requirement of Ofsted to be the responsible person within a registered setting. He also enrolled me on a business course, where I learnt how to carry out market research and make plans for my future venture.

Walking in my purpose carried me to a place of acknowledgement and recognition. For me, my reward was in the children's joy and learning. Their laughter and their energy gave me satisfaction in a job well done, yet those in positions of management offered me a reward that would allow me to shine my light and impact a larger community of children and families. Being the best version of you means you are not cheating yourself or those you are called to impact. I am thankful for all my experiences and have learnt so much from each of them. I continue to grow and only hope that whatever I am led to, I will continue to walk in my calling and my purpose.

Of course, we need remuneration, but the greatest reward is peace of mind and the satisfaction that we achieved what we came to do.

My business plan became my bible. It guided me every step of the way. I used it to receive funding from Waltham Forest and it became my passport into the local primary schools. It outlined our mission statement and how we intended to carry out each point stated. Partnership and making connections were the greatest points of them all. We positioned ourselves as central in the community. We made links with all the local primary schools, the local church, the local authority, and local businesses. Meeting with the schools gave them an overview of the service we were proposing to offer their children. It gave them the ability to signpost parents who were looking for out of school services, as they had the confidence to recommend us. We made it part of our practice to not just *build* connections but to *stay* connected and make our presence known. Collaboration allows all parties to feel they have contributed to the common good. The individuals or organisations that come together with their own expertise can form a partnership and provide a bespoke service. Although we are separate, we are working with the same children and families, therefore it is in our interest to work in support of one another.

Our business proposal was welcomed by all neighbouring schools, but one school allowed us to run a taster session and presentation to prospective parents. We also invited teaching staff to attend. Getting all stakeholders involved is so important in your area of business, as you want them to agree with you, you want them to support you and champion what you do. If they believe in the service, they will recommend your service. If they are sold, they will help to ensure you have longevity and remain viable.

We had several workshops running at the same time, where we set up displays of craft activities children from previous settings had created. We served a variety of fresh fruit and vegetables, as well as savoury sandwiches (food children will be offered during club), and got parents to join in activities that took them back to childhood. Some activities were competitive, others were creative. Everyone got involved and there was so much laughter and positive energy in the room. We took part in a newspaper fashion show where everyone was put into small groups and chose one person as their model. It was the team's job to work together to design and create a unique catwalk stunner within a limited time with newspaper and tape. The fashion show was most certainly the icing on the cake. We had already begun to form our community, the atmosphere screamed 'WE NEED THIS!'

Parents signed their children up there and then, even though we were still yet to secure premises! They enjoyed the feeling of being a part of something greater; it was more than childcare. It was community. It was family. The parents and all other stakeholders who attended had an experience. They didn't just hear a pitch, they were invited to a shared experience, one that the parents themselves enjoyed and would also want their children to participate in.

Because we had the village behind us, with names of children and parents ready to take up our service, the church hall committee felt obliged to offer us the space – the community had spoken! We were able to take the business forward because we rallied all interested parties together. It is important to know that you are creating a solution to an existing problem, or a need that needs to be provided and fulfilled.

It was a great honour to serve local children and families. We became the heart of community as we bridged the schools together. Children of different cultures and different faiths connected under the one ethos of play. The child's right to play was certainly the leading aspect of our service. Our motto became 'WHERE PLAY MATTERS'. The child was always at the heart of everything we did, and the community was built around the child. I had managed to take all my previous experiences, what I had learnt along the way, and pour them into families who stood with us as the wider community. We welcomed and celebrated diversity, allowing individuals and groups to share their culture with us all. This was done through international events where parents would cook their national dishes, music from different parts of the world would be played and even live musicians brought in. We had Irish dancing, Capoeira from the Brazilian community, and African drumming. Our children were provided with a safe space where they could be at one with themselves, helping them to be comfortable with who they were; and to celebrate themselves, by sharing and allowing others to see them with confidence.

The success of any business is measured by what others have to say about you, be it your clientele or your governing body. In our eyes, our clientele were our children. It was the joy on their faces, it was their laughter, it was how engrossed they were in their activities, it was them not wanting to leave when their parents came to collect them. We had one of our young people return after several years, having left for secondary school, to express his gratitude for all we did for him in his younger years. I remember telling him he was going to be the first Black prime minister of the country. He was extremely intelligent, assertive, and strong-minded as a young child. We knew he would go on to achieve greatness. He returned from the boarding school he was attending in Cambridge to share his sentiments about the after-school and holiday clubs he attended. He shared that we helped to form him into the young man he is today. That we allowed him an opportunity to experience the world with varied trips and offsite activities he still remembered like it was yesterday. He said we gave him freedom to express himself and to build his character to become the strong, independent young man he is today. He brought tears to my eyes; he captured all that we had endeavoured to provide.

This was the very reason why our organisation was formed. It was to serve and positively impact the lives of others. Springfield was the foundation. I thought it would only be a part-time job while studying, just a moment passing by. I didn't realise it would go on to help shape the lives of so many children and young people that would come our way.

Running your own business is not a nine to five. There's little to no clocking off as you are the nursing mother to the new baby you have given birth to. You want to make sure all her needs are met, that she is well nurtured and cared for. The sacrifices can be immeasurable as you must make the decision of who and what you are giving your time to. Because you are seeing the manifestation of your vision, you feel you have no choice to give without conditions. You will choose your baby over your partner, your children, extended family, friends, hobbies, and the list goes on… You feel you are abandoning your child if you are not able to fulfil all that is required to be fulfilled. Balance is important, but be assured that like any baby, your business is selfish and self-seeking. It demands your time and in the first few months you may feel you haven't received anything in return. You may become tired and fatigued, struggling to perform in the same capacity as you started, but this it is all normal. You start to find a pattern, probably still giving more than you expected, but it becomes a part of your routine.

I have such a great supportive network of friends and family. A professional mentor has helped keep me focused and on track with forward planning and preparing for the next stages of the business. I noticed that when I did not meet frequently with my mentor, I often felt consumed by the many tasks I had to juggle, and the responsibility of a large team of staff, as well as the children and parents. Accountability is a given, I would recommend and suggest this as a great investment.

In the early stages of business, I found it hard to pull back as I wanted to be involved in all areas of the business. I was on the floor playing with the children; I was a team member, a manager to the team; I liaised with parents, met with professionals, teachers, and head teachers; and had regular catch ups with our company accountant. You soon come to realise you cannot *do* everything and you cannot *be* everything. Delegation is paramount. Recruiting quality staff allows you to feel confident that someone is more than capable of fulfilling a role. It has taken me some time, but I have been able to prioritise my recreation and social time as a necessity for my mental wellbeing. As, although you walk in your purpose, you can still experience burnout if you are not managing your time well and trying to create a work life balance. Exercise has been a central part of my health and wellness routine. This helps me to practise mindfulness and to be fully present in the moment. Only thinking about what I am currently experiencing and not what may have occurred in the workday.

I try to plan an annual family holiday where 100% of our time is dedicated to each other. The children do not have to share me with other children or families, I can be their mum and their mum alone. If I can, a girly holiday is also a must. This is where I can be ME. I am not responsible for another individual but am totally free from playing any role outside of myself.

I am so blessed to have been on this journey and the amazing thing is, it is still unfolding. I know what I have successfully been able to achieve so far, but it continues. You can't hide from purpose, but you can withhold yourself so that you are not walking in it. Obstacles and challenges will come but how willing are you to fulfil your purpose in your community or the world at large? What will your legacy be? Whatever it is you are called to do, how will you impact the lives of others?

Connections cannot and should not be underestimated. Collaboration is powerful and examples have been illustrated throughout this chapter. We all have our strengths and weaknesses. Pulling strengths together allows us to achieve a greater outcome than we would be able to achieve alone. This is a win-win situation for all stakeholders. This includes those delivering the service and those benefitting from the service. You will have to decide in what capacity you would like to involve others in your project or business. Your vision will determine those with whom you choose to travel.

BEC WOODERSON

Bec Wooderson is the founder of Nurturing Numbers.

She offers support and mentoring to self-employed business owners in the UK through her low-cost monthly membership package.

With over 20 years of expertise in accounts software training and mentoring, Bec is often referred to by clients as their 'comfort blanket' and 'sounding board'.

Her passion is helping people gain confidence and clarity with understanding their bookkeeping and accounts in a down-to-earth, fun, and interactive way.

She was nominated for the Women in Accounting 2020 awards, is an AccountingWEB guest expert speaker, has lectured AAT students, and was invited to be a judge at the Practice Excellence Awards.

In her spare time, Bec can often be found in her campervan on a festival site with her crochet, hiking up a hill or having a lazy day at home with her family.

Find out more about Bec:

www.instagram.com/nurturingnumbers

www.nurturingnumbers.co.uk

Nurture Your Numbers – Top Tips for Financial Success

It's an odd feeling for me, writing a chapter in a book by entrepreneurs, for entrepreneurs. You may be wondering why, given that I am here!

Well, the truth of it is, despite having known for quite some time that working for others and being an employee isn't my bag, I feel a bit of an imposter.

I lack the desire to conform to someone else's guidelines or rules... perhaps that's the rebel in me! And if you are on an entrepreneurial journey, I would encourage you to embrace that rebel in you too!

How did I end up here?

I've been reflecting on how I ended up here.

Not only looking back at my working life, but even as far back as my high school and sixth form years, to try and understand for myself why the journey to becoming an entrepreneur was always something I was destined to take, even if I didn't realise it until much later in life.

Perhaps you've been wondering how you ended up here, too?

Maybe like me, you also kind of just fell into doing what you do now as a career.

I didn't purposefully choose this path to start with – I had wanted to be an architect! I guess you could say it found me or perhaps I was always destined to do this, but just didn't realise it at the time.

I got a grade B for GCSE Maths at high school and I wouldn't say that I've ever been particularly good at mental arithmetic – pass me my calculator even for the simplest of sums... it's like an appendage I can't live without!

But, here I am...

One failed A Level.

One change in options.

Zero direction.

No clue what I really wanted to do.

Yet, I have been running a successful bookkeeping agency and accounts software training business since 2007 and supporting business owners who want to do their own accounts in-house.

I have:

- a team of 16 incredible humans I call my work family;

- amazing clients;

- drive in spades;

- passion in bucket loads; and

- a desire to help others.

Actually, when it boils down to it, I have always wanted to help others.

My friends always used to call me 'Mummy Bec', and so in my voyage of self-discovery as to why I was always destined to become an entrepreneur, I messaged a school friend to ask why they called me this and these were some parts of her reply that stood out:

"Because you were able to make that kind of empathic leap into someone else's shoes."

"You very much cared about what someone was experiencing and wanted to make that experience better for them."

"It was about care and support and making sure the outcomes for people were just a bit better in some way."

"You made it your mission to improve that situation for them using your resources and insights and empathy."

It's interesting that when I read those back and think of my fellow female entrepreneurial friends and peers, everyone I can think of (and I mean everyone), also has these attributes.

So, perhaps we're a particular breed. Perhaps we all have the same attributes but just different areas of expertise, and that's what makes us entrepreneurs.

My advice to you

Being a business owner, an entrepreneur, a CEO (or whatever title you decide to give yourself), is rewarding but hard work.

Having trained and mentored business owners with their accounts since 2000, it will probably come as no surprise to you that my advice is about how to avoid the mistakes I've seen business owners make time and time again. And how you can ensure you don't make the same mistakes yourself.

My top three tips are:

1) **Stay on top of your bookkeeping**

2) **Ensure your taxes are paid on time**

3) **Make sure it's worth your while financially and pay yourself**

I know, I know… I said taxes! Cue lots of you promptly moving onto the next chapter of the book!

But bear with me…

If there's one thing most new business owners fear, it's getting things wrong with the authorities. Not knowing what they should be doing, when they should be doing it or getting details wrong.

Basically, insert any kind of worry/fear/anxious emotion here and you get the gist!

Let me tell you this…

It doesn't need to be scary.

It doesn't need to be something you dread or worry about.

It's just about getting the right support and guidance to give you confidence.

That could be either:

- The confidence of knowing it's been taken care of by someone else by outsourcing it to a bookkeeping agency; or

- Having a mentor to help you devise an action plan, know your deadlines and timeframes, and hold you accountable and keep you on track.

How would it make you feel knowing you could fall into one of these two camps and never miss a beat?

And…relax.

I mentioned staying on top of your bookkeeping.

When I say this, I mean one of three things depending on your situation, to avoid you falling into a trap I've seen repeated many times over by business owners:

a) You are doing your own accounts

b) You employ someone else to do it

c) You outsource it

Let's look at these in turn.

a) You are doing your own accounts

Please. Please, please…if you're a sole trader and filing your own tax return – don't leave it until 31st January and pour yourself a large glass of wine and 'tackle the books'!

It is so much less stressful to keep on top of it regularly and know everything is in order ready for submission.

Did you know that business owners who know their numbers are much more likely to make more money? As the saying goes, 'Where our attention goes, energy flows'.

This is the exact reason I set up my membership, as being a business owner can be a lonely place.

If accounts:

- fill you with fear;

- make you bury your head in the sand; or

- mean you constantly put it off…

If every year you wish you'd done things differently, having a mentor and community of fellow business owners to keep you on track and hold you accountable is just the tonic you need.

b) You employ someone else to do it

Now this is a biggie!

I have lost count of the number of times I've helped clients pick themselves out of a mess, as the person they employed to do their accounts didn't know what they were doing. Anyone can tell you they are good at bookkeeping or accounts.

But the proof is in the pudding!

If you're recruiting, make sure you ask relevant questions around their qualification to do the job well and question them about their skills and experience if you can.

There is a free 'Accounts Staff Screening Questions' checklist on our Nurturing Numbers website at www.nurturingnumbers.co.uk if it's helpful for you.

Bear in mind, a person with the right attributes and skill set can be trained to be a good bookkeeper, and sometimes it does come down to the right person being a good fit, who, with your support and guidance, can excel at the bookkeeping role.

If you're a business owner who plans to employ someone in-house to do your bookkeeping or accounts, I'd recommend you take adequate measures to ensure they are suitably skilled to do the job.

If you're not confident to ask number or figure related questions yourself, see if you can find someone that is, to give you another angle during the selection process.

In some cases you may feel a skills assessment is prudent. When I've done these in the past and presented them to employers of prospective candidates they have been very revealing!

Remember, if you're employing someone to do the accounts, it is you that is ultimately responsible for the accuracy of those numbers as the business owner.

Larger businesses may require a set of audited accounts, but as a member of the board you still carry responsibilities to ensure the accounts are accurate.

c)   You outsource it

Should you decide to outsource your bookkeeping, do your research. Don't be afraid to take up references for the individual or firm you decide to use.

If they are a member of a professional bookkeeping or accountancy body, ask to see their certificates.

Making sure you get proof of their professional indemnity insurance is also recommended. This insurance protects you if the work or advice the bookkeeper or accountant gives you means you suffer any financial loss, for example.

Asking to see that they have this insurance cover in place shows them you are taking things seriously and are being thorough by doing your due diligence.

You want to ensure they have the necessary things in place to give you peace of mind.

> There's a handy checklist of the things I recommend you obtain from any bookkeeper or accountant you are looking to engage on our website www.nurturingnumbers.co.uk.

When choosing a bookkeeper, if that person is a sole practitioner, I'd recommend you ask the bookkeeper who would cover your accounts if they became unwell or were unable to work. It's tricky to have that kind of conversation if the need ever arose, so having it as one of your fact-finding questions means there's no awkward conversation to be had at a later date.

Regardless of which option you choose and how your accounts are done, I'd recommend you know your numbers throughout your year.

I know so many business owners who only ever know their annual profits and tax due when their accountant has prepared their year-end or they do their own tax return.

All digital bookkeeping software allows you to see how much profit you've made at the click of a button.

If someone else is doing your books, make sure you're in regular contact with them to go over how things are looking and ask any questions you're not sure about.

Knowing your numbers and keeping a close eye on the detail regularly is amazing for focusing your mind and energy on your financials.

Four reasons businesses fail

By far the biggest mistakes I see business owners make which hurt their businesses are:

1. Thinking that as there is money in the business, it's all mine... right?!

2. Thinking cash equals profits (or vice-versa!)

3. Not knowing where they are spending their hard-earned cash

4. Failing to understand their cashflow

Let's look at each of these in turn:

1. Thinking that as there is money in the business, it's all mine... right?!

Wrong! One of the most common reasons businesses fail is that people take out more money than they should.

If you have £10,000 in your bank account, it isn't necessarily all yours to take.

Without getting too technical here, what you want to do is consider what else needs to be paid out of that pot of money.

For example:

- Suppliers who have sent you an invoice you've not yet paid

- A monthly loan repayment, if you have one

- A bit for tax on the profits you've made

- Monthly memberships or subscriptions, e.g. Canva, networking fees

If you are a Limited Company there are other considerations too.

If you are not doing your accounts yourself, I'd recommend you ask the person doing it so you are confident you know where you stand.

If you are doing your own bookkeeping, make sure you have someone you can turn to if you're not sure about something and need to gain confidence and clarity on a situation.

2. Thinking cash equals profits (or vice-versa!)

Cash doesn't always equal profits.

If your bank balance is looking healthy, it doesn't always mean your profits are. And vice-versa, your profit on paper might look great, but you may not be swimming in cash.

Perhaps you have had a great sales month and invoiced your clients on say, 31st March, so the March accounts are looking fantastic, but those clients still owe you that money into April.

There are two financial reports you want to become familiar with:

Profit & Loss Statement

It does what it says on the tin – shows you whether your business has made a profit or a loss in a particular date range.

More costs than sales and you've made a loss.

More sales than costs and you've made a profit.

It's that simple!

Balance Sheet Statement

This shows how healthy your business is at any given point in time. Think of it as taking a photo on the last day of every month to see how things look in each snapshot in time.

What things affect how healthy your business is on your Balance Sheet?

Good things are, for example:

- Assets you own

- Cash in your bank account

- The amount of money your customers owe you

Bad things are, for example:

- An overdrawn bank account

- Any money you owe to your suppliers

- Taxes you owe

Once you have grasped these two financial statements, it will make understanding your accounts a lot easier.

When I teach and mentor, I often refer to learning accounts much like doing a puzzle. We start with the four corners, then the edges and finally fill in the middle and build up the picture from there.

3.   Not knowing where they are spending their hard-earned cash

Do you suffer with shiny object syndrome? I know I do!

When was the last time you went through your company credit card statement or looked at what goes through your accounts, to ask yourself if you need that piece of software or subscription?

Or whether you're really making use of the software you're paying for.

I regularly do this with our own accounts and the last time I did it, I saved over £1,200 a year by cancelling things we were paying for but never using.

And that could be money you'd like to invest elsewhere, or it could be money you need to save.

Heck, it could end up in your own pocket!

This exercise is so beneficial and one I regularly take my members through, as it enables you to keep your finger on the pulse and feel in control.

4. Failing to understand their cashflow

If you had no cash coming in over the next 30, 60 or 90 days – do you know how much cash you would need to cover your regular outgoings?

Scary thought, huh?!

Whilst we hope this will never happen, it's good to know what this figure is, so you feel more in control and can even start to build up a cash buffer if you don't already have one, to give yourself something to fall back on if you ever need it.

This is cashflow. It is the flow of money and making sure you have the right amount in your account at the right time. It is something that all business owners need to understand.

Top tips for financial success

1. Pay yourself what you deserve

As a business owner myself, I understand that we invest to further our business for future success.

I see clients so stressed, working long hours and feeling resentful that their staff are getting paid more than them. They question if they should just call it quits and go and get a job, and I can't help but want to sit them down and 'work everything backwards'.

What do I mean by 'work everything backwards'?

Well… what is it you want to take home? £1,000, £3,000, £10,000 a month? What is that number for you?

Grab a piece of paper and set that intention. Put it on a vision or gratitude board if that kind of thing floats your boat.

Now, we need to work backwards. I find using a spreadsheet helps as it will do all the calculations for you!

Starting with the figure you want in your pocket every month, what do we need to add back to arrive at the sales figure you need (if you are VAT registered, ignore any VAT for this exercise)?

Factor in everything you can think of, plus a contingency fund in case you splurge on something you weren't expecting.

And if you're not sure what you need to add back, as you aren't sure what your costs or overheads are, then this is absolutely one the reasons you need to do this exercise!

For example:

If you want to take home £3,000, you need to add to this the costs you have each month to arrive at your sales target. Don't forget to add in some for tax too!

Take home	£3,000

Add:

Software subscription	£12
Insurance	£60
Stationery & Printing	£79
Networking	£49
Bookkeeper	£100
Tax	£900

Your sales target would be	£4,200

N.B. *All figures are fictitious and totally made up!*

Knowledge is power…

There is so much I could say on the topic of keeping on top of your accounts and nurturing your numbers, but that's for another time!

2. Surround yourself with cheerleaders and those with complementary skills

Wow, if I could have told myself this 10 years ago, I'd have got to where I am now so much quicker!

I was chatting to my sister recently about friendships.

I was saying that as I get older, the friendships I have formed have changed over time. They are now kind of 'clusters' based on shared experiences, e.g. NCT group, school friends, work colleagues, uni mates etc.

Once you become a business owner, I can hands-down say that finding your 'tribe' (or whatever you want to call it) is **the** best thing. A place where you can share the highs and lows of running a business, no matter what stage you are at.

It's true to say that your friends and acquaintances who are business owners can relate to you on a totally different level. It can give you the space to discuss the challenges we face and the celebrations too.

It could be a late-night WhatsApp message to celebrate the award you just got nominated for. It could be the friend who reaches out and needs to chat about how frantic they are and needs guidance on how they can cope with their increased workload.

I certainly think there's a common misconception that if you are overworked and stretched as a busy business owner, you need to clone yourself (that was certainly what I thought for a long time!).

But actually, the opposite was true for me.

I didn't need another me. I needed people to complement my skills and attributes, to take over doing the stuff I didn't enjoy or, quite frankly, wasn't good at!

And these people don't need to be employed. You could outsource to a VA, hire a sub-contractor or even outsource to an agency.

The best thing I ever did in 2021 was list all the things I was doing day-to-day that were time consuming that someone else could do and ask them to take those tasks from me.

I was guilty of doing things myself to 'just get it done' or because 'it's quicker if I do it, as I'll only have to show someone'.

It was such a liberating exercise.

There was a tonne of admin on that list that I really didn't need to be doing, and was actually taking me away from what I should have been focusing on, which meant I was having to work evenings and weekends to get the other stuff done!

Does any of this resonate with you or sound familiar?

Now, I always ask myself, "What could I be doing with that time if I didn't have to do task X, Y or Z? Is there anyone else that could do it besides me if they had some training and guidance?"

Yes, it would take some planning and time to explain what to do or show them the ropes, but it would free me up to focus on what I enjoy and build the business.

3. Don't be afraid to ask for help and guidance

Just ask.

You'll feel better for it and it will equip you with more tools for your tool box, that one day may even be able to help others.

In my teens and twenties, I was always the person that bottled things up and didn't want to talk about things that were bothering me, until it got to the point where it all just got a bit too much and it 'all came out'!

I used to think that asking for help was a weakness.

Help and guidance doesn't have to be paid for. It can be a free community of people who 'get you'; it can be a helping hand if you need something sorting; it might be an online resource someone can point you towards.

More than this, asking for help or guidance is a courageous thing to do. It teaches us that admitting our weaknesses is a good thing, and something we should normalise every day.

Ask yourself, "What do you need help with?"

Do you need guidance in making a decision? Perhaps you're unsure if you should be a Limited Company or VAT registered?

Are you looking to recruit your first team member? Maybe you need guidance on your responsibilities as an employer and what you need to do about pension auto-enrolment?

Would you like to make sure you are turning a profit before your accountant does your year-end, but aren't quite sure what you need to do to find out?

Maybe you want to increase your earnings and need to look at where you can save money or increase revenue in your business, but need some input.

Perhaps you've got some big projects coming up and need a hand with forecasting your cashflow, but need a steer on how to do it and what to consider.

Whatever help and guidance you need, there is help out there.

In order to get it, you just need to ask or go and seek it out.

What has helped me in my journey to being an entrepreneur?

Is it inappropriate to say wine, chocolate and long working hours?!

Seriously (and I had to think about this one long and hard), there are three things:

1.   Treating others as I would want to be treated

I love a good surprise just like the next person. So whether that's a call to a client as I know they've had a tough time lately, or a box of brownies in the post to my team for being awesome.

The small things and thoughtful gestures really do go a long way.

2. Pushing myself out of my comfort zone

In my early twenties I wanted the world to swallow me whole.

There I stood, in a room full of 50 or so people at a networking meeting – dry mouth, sweaty palms, sure I was going to fumble over my words. I wanted nothing more than to sit in the corner and people watch.

But looking back, this experience was one of self-development and helped me gain the confidence I needed, I just didn't realise it at the time.

People even say to me now, would I be nervous standing up in front of a room full of people and talking? Because I've been put in these positions (yes, often thrown in the deep end!), where I've been completely out of my comfort zone and, quite frankly, shitting myself, by having to talk in front of complete strangers, the answer is no, I wouldn't be nervous.

3. People I've met along the way

Looking back, I realise the people I've met along the way have made a huge difference to my business and to me personally. They helped me gain the confidence I needed to become a better leader and a greater mentor.

Not only have they helped me gain positives, but they have also helped me let go of the negative things that were holding me back, such as self-sabotage, perfectionism, lack of self-worth and low confidence.

For this I am forever grateful.

No matter where you are on your entrepreneurial journey, find your people.

Don't hold back.

Be yourself.

HELEN JOHNSON

Helen Johnson is a coach, EFT/NLP therapist, and coach trainer on a quest to bring people great coaching and personal development without the BS.

She founded Coaching Beyond, offering ICF coach training and continued professional development, to help people to help themselves AND others to make the most of their strengths and find fulfilment in work and life.

A force to be reckoned with and a maverick spirit, she has a rich and diverse professional background including a PhD in how to help transform people's lives, a philosophy degree from the University of Oxford, and a previous career as a barrister.

Find out more at:

www.coachingbeyondhub.com and www.linktr.ee/helenbjohnson

Knight in Shining Armour Syndrome

I once spent an entire networking party telling people how my surname is slang for 'penis' in the States. Don't ask me why. I'm not even sure myself. In the end, I simply pretended to go to the loo and then slid along the wall out of sight and down the stairs. All very dignified, eh? I'm sure they teach that at Harvard Business School. On balance, I'd say I am not naturally inclined to successful networking.

Luckily nowadays I hang out with people in a community that a) can laugh along with me about these things and b) values and respects me despite the fact I can't be trusted to hold a polite conversation. Total win!

In fact, a strange thing has been happening recently. I keep getting thank you emails. This is very confusing to me because...

Firstly, I'm enjoying myself, so how can that be work? And secondly, most confusing of all, I keep being myself with these clients. How the bloody hell am I getting away with it?!

In the most recent cohort that I am training in ICF Coaching, there are people who have spent thousands of pounds on previous training and are commanding extremely high fees. I worried about what they'd get out of my course beyond the formal qualification. And guess what? They are being challenged and learning loads. Better still, there isn't an ounce of BS in sight. We have fun and talk to each other like normal human beings. Same goes for my one-to-one clients as a coach and EFT therapist.

I love it.

But, there is a small part of me that sometimes whispers, "Maybe I should be less me and more…" (*fill in the blank with any number of things I think I 'should' be*). I have to tell that part of me not to be a dick.

Because it wasn't (and sometimes still isn't) always like this. Comfortable. Enjoyable. Feeling like I'm really making an impact.

My career has largely been characterised by something else entirely. Something I call 'the knight in shining armour' syndrome that ultimately took me far away from myself. I'll tell you all about that later. For now, I have stories to tell…

I was a pupil barrister (this means a trainee trial lawyer) and my supervisor was helping a not-so-lovely and oh-so-stereotypical man take his wife to the cleaners having run off with the secretary (I kid you not). Now, this could have been a proper love story and he could well have been in a bad marriage, and I might have chosen to believe this if the words coming out of his mouth weren't a constant stream of sexist drivel. After the whole ordeal was over, we went to the pub, whereby the following conversation occurred:

Man: "So… Does she (nodding in my direction) want to do what you do then?"

Supervisor: "Yes."

Man: "Noooo. She's too (gestures to my face) liberal with her mouth."

Supervisor: "Well, I have told her that."

Now. This was indeed fair comment. However, the truth of this statement is not what we are here to discuss. I want to draw attention to my reaction to it. Oh, I was crushed. I had really, really wanted this supervisor to stick up for me, believing his opinion was the opinion of the entire legal system and therefore indicative of my entire value in terms of my career.

What I should have been thinking was 'Wow, you two are rude AF'. What I should have been telling myself was that there is no possible world in which it is ok for two men to be talking about me as if I am a doorknob instead of a human being capable of conversation. That belittling others is not ok and there is no good reason for it. And they should be aware that one of them is in a position of power over me. On every level this interaction was a massive no. But instead? I thought I deserved it. And I also felt completely untethered, because I believed that I needed that supervisor's approval to succeed in life.

Maybe we could put this down to being young and impressionable. Yet, fast forward a number of years and I'm sitting in front of my computer desperately trying not to laugh. I've got two fingers pushing my cheeks in to try and disguise my face and make it look like I am being 'thoughtful'. At this point, if I don't laugh, I will cry. I'm not sure which would have been easier to disguise?!

If the 'presentation' (read: company-wide bollocking) I was watching had honest subtitles it would say 'I would be a millionaire by now if it wasn't for you useless bastards that I have to manage all the time'. At one point, a picture of a sad face appears. This is the point I can no longer keep a straight face.

I'm trying to process. Is this normal? The gaslighting? The reprimands (often public)? The arbitrary rules imposed and then retracted? One minute you are the golden child, the next you have a target on your back? The drama? I don't know how to describe the work environment (well, not without revealing too many juicy details, anyway!). All I can say is that it was one of those places that shook your spirit, even when you couldn't quite put your finger on why.

Actually, it wasn't funny at all. In this company, people got hurt. Repeatedly. I surreptitiously texted my colleague. She had been on holiday. 'How does it feel to be back?' 'I just threw up,' she replied. Over time, more and more people would come out of the woodwork to share their stories with me. Almost every one of them would turn it a little bit on themselves. 'I thought it was me, I lost so much confidence', 'I don't know why this is upsetting me so much', 'I am so shocked'. It hurt to hear this because I knew none of it was their fault and that this pattern had a life of its own.

In both situations above, I wasn't quite clear on how I'd got there. I felt like a lion who had been mistaken for a gerbil, albeit sometimes a gerbil that came in handy. I felt completely unseen, and completely divorced from…well, reality! Yet, the messages about my incompetence were creeping into my consciousness. I started to feel 'wrong' somehow. Maybe if I just played the game a little bit better? Pleased them more? I could just keep my head down… But I couldn't. Lions are gonna lion. So, both situations ended with me uprooting myself from my security and taking a different path.

When it came to my career, I hadn't been afraid to do the unconventional or take risks. I had taken a pretty prestigious path at first – University of Oxford, becoming a barrister – and then I had veered completely off course and gone rogue. Travelled. Did a lot of yoga. That kind of thing. I worked in charities and then I did a PhD, but I did not settle into anything sensible. I went freelance. I REFUSED to do what was 'safe'. I even got fired from one place (now that was an embarrassing day).

There was a part of me that was very brave. Yet there was also a part of me that kept falling into powerlessness. Along the way I had learnt many things, but NOT how to fully trust and believe in myself and my own power – and this meant that I frequently gave it away, even in the face of glaringly bad behaviour, but also in more subtle ways too.

I had made an Olympic sport of creating 'knights in shining armour' in my own mind. There was always someone for me to hand over my salvation to. Always a mentor, a guru, a contact, an organisation, a platform, a connection that would help to raise me up. This wasn't the only realm in which I did this – I did it in relationships too. The amount of LIFE that I had wasted waiting for some guy (who – shock, horror – never actually turned out to be THE guy) to give me the love and attention I craved.

When I first started as an EFT therapist (I'm now also a coach and coach trainer), there was one organisation that took an interest in me. Unbeknownst to them I latched onto them in my mind as the lord and saviour of my burgeoning career. I did barely anything constructive to raise my own profile while I waited for them to follow through on some promise they had made me (I don't even remember what it was – featuring me on this thing or that thing, something like that). I thought that once they shone a light on me then people would see me… But it didn't even occur to me that I could shine a light on myself.

I'd done it with other things too. Job opportunities that I thought were coming, mentors who advised me to create this product or that product but then wouldn't endorse it. Networking groups I thought would help me expand if I just sat in them and – I don't know – lured attendees in with my sexual magnetism?! I don't know! I just know that I always thought there would be a solution outside of me. One solution that came from someone who had more power than me.

I knew I had talent, but I fundamentally did not believe I had any power at all (I would have scoffed if you had told me this though!). You might have called it 'fear of success', 'imposter syndrome' or 'not having a marketing background', but what it really, fundamentally was, was that I always thought someone or something had the power to get me what I wanted in a way I simply couldn't do alone.

In a way I was right. Because NONE of us do life successfully alone. We are, at our core, completely interdependent. Independence is a myth. I didn't invent Wi-Fi, did I?! I don't fetch water every day. And I certainly don't grow my regular oat milk honeycomb lattes on trees in my back garden (please excuse my wanky – but delicious – coffee choices). All of us, all of the time, are working together. Yet somehow, I had failed to realise the essential difference between investing all my power in mythical knights in shining armour and actually getting out into the world, building connections, building a business and being my own knight in shining armour!

And there was something even worse.

I am pathologically honest, real, unceremonious – I do not go in for fakery, BS, and unnecessary formalities. One of my superpowers is getting people to relax and focus on the real shit, not the irrelevant peripheries. You'd think I was always being myself. But somewhere along the road, while working in a toxic environment, I started to realise I had become a liar. I lied to everyone around me because I didn't want to leave my job due to stability/finances. I wasn't about to put 'help me, I'm working for a maniac' on my email signature! I lied to MYSELF about the impact it was having on me, and I lied to my boss and my colleagues over and over to avoid any more drama (often resulting in more). I was being…. Fake. The shame! Fear will do that to you.

Once I started looking around me, I saw these fear-based behaviours happening all over the place. Happening to bad ass, kind, wonderful people… Many of whom were also carrying wounds from people they had tried to make *their* knights in shining armour.

Here's what I saw – do you recognise anything here?

- Buying someone's service because you really (secretly) want to be them or have their success and not for the substance of the product itself.

- Hanging on to connections or communities for dear life, even when something feels off, because you think they have something you need, or you have put them on a pedestal.

- Everything suddenly being about whether you are above or below someone else – status games galore.

- Thinking that money and your value are the same thing, instead of money simply being a resource you deserve to have more of. And so, having less than others makes you feel less than as a person.

- Believing that you are 'bad' at things and this has to be because of some major flaw, instead of just something you haven't yet mastered.

- Sometimes only investing in 'strategy' because it sounds 'businessy' but not investing in your own learning or wellbeing, because f**k my skills and resources, I just need to be told what to do!

- Hiding all the best bits about you and struggling to perform as a version of yourself that you deem 'acceptable' and 'businessy' but feels disconnected.

- Perhaps also completely abandoning a previous version of yourself and attempting a total reinvention, not realising you are throwing the baby out with the bath water...

- Being disillusioned and abandoning the industry you love because of painful experiences.

Fear and self-abandonment are extremely addictive. They are also extremely seductive and manipulative. They will convince you that you need them. They will even convince you that they are helping you! But I was coming to realise that either I learnt to raise MYSELF up, or I was going to hand over my power to lunatics forever. So, I was going to put on my big girl pants and start taking a new approach to life. Easy! Good job I always set myself nice simple goals, eh?

To be honest, I'm not here to tell you a success story, because this is a work in progress. I'm not yet a massive guru (hard to believe, I know). I can't wow you with numbers – money, followers, and the like. But this is precisely why it's important that we talk about this now. Because it shouldn't be about how you do or don't get to success. It should be about how you don't care what the outcome is, because your fundamental sense of YOU and your power is not going to be up for compromise.

Is this also a recipe for success?? Of course it bloody is. Let me tell you why:

No one is going to be your knight in shining armour, and if they look like they are then they are probably about to try to kidnap you and put you at the top of a very tall tower, which if nothing else, is going to bore the crap out of you (or worse).

So, what are you – we – going to do instead?

The theme of this book is connection. So, we are going to explore: how do I connect and keep my own power? How do I connect joyously and avoid the connections that suck me dry? How do I do this as fully myself and still feel safe?

As you can imagine, I have been thinking about this a lot, and because I am very generous, I will share my thoughts with you. Or what I like to call, 'Helen's grand plan to no longer be a dick to herself (and now yours too)':

1.   Oh my God, you are so freaking epic and everyone wants you!

Imagine if I told you there is absolutely no room for a real, kind, clever, impactful person who stands in their integrity in your industry. No one wants that. It is completely unwelcome. People like that are completely worthless. Sounds a bit ridiculous, doesn't it?

I bet you want it! I bet when you look back on times you have been disappointed in life and business, that was *exactly* what you wanted. Imagine someone came to you and said, "Well, I have to act like I'm on The Apprentice and be a total pestilence on society otherwise I'll never make any money!" I'm sure some poor misguided fool has already said that to you actually, because it is a popular belief. However, it is also complete claptrap. One of my friends is a really big deal at a really big bank. You know what he said to me the other day? I find you get further by being nice.

Good people are wanted! They are craved! And if you are not around to be both skilful and truly good natured then who else is going to be there? Just the unethical people with their smoke and mirrors.

There is space for you. You are welcome. You are valued. Keep creating opportunities for people to value you.

Also, of course, as much as I am advocating not being a dick, we all are sometimes. That's ok too. Learn from it, make amends if you need to, develop any skills that are required moving forward, and then let it go. You have to bring your whole self at all times. That includes the parts you are trying to ignore or reject. Let yourself be aware of them and love yourself anyway. Let yourself off the hook.

2.   Toxic people are toxic.

Let this be your first rule of life and business: I am surrounded by good people, and I am good to myself.

Here's the thing. Toxic people's toxicity will always creep in. I know many people who have chosen to overlook this because of the 'opportunity' or because they 'need the money', or even just to be kind to the person and give them the benefit of the doubt. In fact, I have witnessed people get an increasing sense of unease around a toxic person without knowing why – not knowing they are in the presence of a snake, and the reason they feel a bit funny or 'wrong' is because the life, confidence, joy, and energy is being subtly drained from them. Sometimes they come to realise later what was really going on. Sadly, sometimes they go for years thinking something was up with them. Maybe they are not good enough or don't fit in? You know the kind of crap we tell ourselves! What I've learnt from toxic people is they will take. No matter what you think they offer, all that will happen is you will be drained.

However, it's not always an easy call, is it? We can't very well jump ship from every connection just because something feels off. Relationships DO take work and compromise, after all. It's an art form, a balancing act. Here are a few guidelines:

1.   Listen to yourself. You know. The signs are there. Stay tuned in. Respect your intuition and bring in boundaries.

2.   On the other hand, you carry a lot of crap as well. There could be some 'you' stuff going on. Allow for the possibility of it being a 'them' thing while also allowing that it might be a 'you' thing.

3.   Are you expecting this person to rescue you in some way? If so, take that obligation back and start rescuing yourself IMMEDIATELY. Do NOT give anyone else the power.

The fastest way to build connections that really work for you is to go for the community that feels good to you – opportunity will always be there. There will always be fruitful connections. Your connections will flourish when you genuinely know, like, and respect the people you are surrounded by. Trust yourself to grow a circle of the right people, not the 'ought to' people.

Nevertheless, be careful. Sometimes what feels 'good' might just be 'safe'. Diversity in our communities is so core. It helps to keep our own selves fresh and challenged, and it helps to keep what you create together innovative and impactful. So never mistake 'comfort' for 'right'.

Go for the most exciting, vibrant, lovely, interesting people – go where you really mean it. That kind of genuine bond is magnetic.

3. Be about 3000% more lazy.

Please, please, do not compromise on quality. However, for everything else, give yourself a bloody break!

You can trust yourself. You don't have to poke and prod at yourself, constantly fight fires, troubleshoot, and correct your course. You can let things be. The single best piece of advice known to humankind is simply this: detach from the outcome. This doesn't mean to no longer have goals or values. It means to decide who you want to be, focus on your core values and be led by them, stay in integrity, have fun and be playful, experiment, and then... let go.

Don't 'try' to be yourself. Just actually be yourself. Don't convince, persuade, or constantly seek approval. Instead, trust that you, just as you are, in your natural state, is enough to be impressive. No more compromising to fit into the mould of who you 'think' you should be. No more performing a version of yourself that is either not you at all or is a kind of exaggerated, mega version of you (because otherwise people won't see or understand unless you shout about it!). No more compare and despair – where you look at other people and pick apart all the ways you don't live up to their greatness. You get into true alignment, and you are just... You.

Boundaries are an important part of this. Being 3000% more lazy means having bloody good boundaries that protect you from BS. However, instead of being walls that are used to protect you from shame ('Oh I won't share that because it makes me look bad!'), these boundaries become about mutual respect and being tuned into your own energy and that of other people. No one wants to see your bare arse plonked on the edge of the dinner table while they are eating, do they?! (Well, I'm sure some might). Being you isn't about letting it all hang out with no awareness of others... We keep good boundaries to create a great energy for everyone and to make things a whole lot more relaxed.

So, there you have it.

I realise that I am writing this as if I follow these guidelines perfectly at all times. I do not. Some are easier than others. I find the boundaries thing particularly tricky, and I constantly battle with the 'being myself' thing, finding that I always feel too much or too little. Sometimes I would prefer to take a nap than even think about having to follow any of them – far easier and I can't get into any trouble! However, what I can guarantee is that these rules really will keep you in your power. Even if you do them imperfectly, which is actually part of giving yourself a break. They prevent the knight in shining armour syndrome from getting a foothold, and where it does creep in, they help you to let it go again. I started doing the knight in shining armour idea again recently and had to remind myself of my own advice! It was easier this time to shake myself out of it.

Lastly, when you are following these rules, you might care less about success… but it will come anyway.

KYLIE CARTER

Kylie is a spiritual mentor and white witch, working with soulful ladies, encouraging them to live in alignment with their higher selves; healing from past (or past life) trauma, connecting with Spirit, and exploring their life purpose.

As a psychic medium, Reiki Master and Akashic Records specialist, Kylie encourages you to release what no longer serves you and stand within your power, creating the life you want. All too often, women follow a path that society tells them they 'should'. But their beautiful light is desperate to shine through, if they'll only allow it.

Armed with divination tools, connection with Spirit, and blessings from Mother Gaia and the Moon, Kylie would love to help you step into the full power of you.

Find out more at msha.ke/confidencecoven/

You Are Never Alone

"With the right alignment, everything you want makes its way into your experience. You are the keeper of your own gate."

— Esther Hicks

During the hustle and bustle of business and trying to achieve the countless unrealistic goals I was setting for myself, it took me a long time to realise that alignment and being true to yourself is the real key to success. I learnt the freedom, joy and importance of just being myself. After all, it's the only one true thing we can master in this lifetime, but that isn't where my journey of spirituality began...

I was just a child when spirituality came to play a key role in my life, and whilst I may have been too young to appreciate it at the time, I now realise the pivotal part it played in who I became (and who I'll hopefully evolve into). My beautiful mum had multiple sclerosis, but this didn't stop all the fun and laughter in the house as I was growing up. She was prescribed a concoction of drugs and pain relief, but this wore off after a while. The one thing she swore by was Reiki energy healing.

I remember watching in awe as a child as my mum lay still and a kind man came and laid pretty stones all over her body, and seemingly made her feel better. I mean, wow! We had a magical man coming to our house to perform miracles, it doesn't get much cooler than that.

My mum also spoke quite openly and regularly about how, as she lost the sight in her eyes, it was replaced by beautiful colours. She may no longer be able to see people's physical features too well, but she could see the colour of what I now know to be their aura. And this special ability gave her an insight into their intent and helped to aid her intuition.

Unfortunately, my mum passed when I was a child, which was devastating. I had lost my whole world as I knew it, and with her went my connection to the spiritual world. I didn't really know anyone else who believed in receiving guidance and healing from above. I didn't really know anyone who could see colours around people and knew what they represented, and being a child, you can imagine how well that went down in the school playground. So, I learned to suppress those beliefs and feelings, and they were pushed deep down. I became a pro at wearing my mask, to protect my true self.

That feeling of being 'different' never went away, though. I found myself just *knowing* things that others didn't, but I didn't know how or why. I would get 'gut feelings' about people and situations, but being a child and teenager, I ignored these (and then learnt to regret it). I still found myself attracted to crystals and tarot/oracle cards, and I always had the most vivid dreams. But it wasn't 'cool' (which was my number one priority growing up), and so I continued to ignore what my intuition was telling me and focused my attention on boys and parties instead...

...Until the day something unexplainable, profound and beautiful happened, and it happened on what may have been the very darkest of my days!

At the age of 20, my beautiful one-year-old daughter gave me the strength to leave an abusive relationship. More than that, she empowered me to stand against my abuser in court – to fight for freedom for both of us. Whilst I was being torn apart during the cross-examination, there was a moment that I felt like giving up. I hadn't allowed my family to come to court as I didn't want them to have to listen to the ins and outs of everything this man had done to me. I felt the most alone I had felt in a long time, perhaps ever.

And then it happened. I could feel my mum swoop me up in her arms and surround me with more strength and love than I had ever felt. I KNEW she was right there with me, supporting me. For the first time in 10 years, I could feel her standing next to me. And I knew I couldn't give up – I knew I had to continue fighting for me and my baby girl. And most importantly, I KNEW I had never been alone, all this time.

I went on to win the court battle and continued to have the strength to fight. Knowing I wasn't alone ignited something within me. I didn't even realise that not only did I have my mum, but I had my whole team of spirit guides cheering me on and guiding me!

I continued to talk to my mum and feel her presence daily. It was no longer a 'wanting' or a 'wishing' – it was an undeniable *knowing* for me. But it wasn't until 2020 that I realised helping others along their spiritual journey was my calling. When the world went into shock at the start of the pandemic, I decided to do something for my own health and cut down on drinking. This was the point that I actually thought I could be going insane! I was receiving messages thick and fast from Spirit and didn't have a clue what was happening. I could feel myself changing and transforming, but it was terrifying because I didn't understand it.

Spirit decided to lend me a helping hand by placing my first spiritual teacher, Clare Liza, in my path, and I felt so very drawn to this beautiful lady. She was closely followed by another amazing and inspirational lady and my Reiki Master, Clair Anderson. I now recognise this feeling of being drawn to someone as a sign from my Higher Self that this person is here to help guide or teach me in some way and they're in my life for a reason. These ladies helped me unpick the layers, slow down the messages from Spirit so I could absorb the information, connect with universal life force energy for healing, and they taught me to hone the skill of connecting with my guides. From the very first day of learning, I was hooked and haven't stopped learning since.

Extremely early on in this process I knew helping ladies connect with their spiritual side and align with their souls was my calling. I then reached the point that I could look back over my work and business life and could see the common thread that tied everything together. Perhaps there was a similarity in my 'Jack of all trades' history! I had trained as a counsellor, and then after working with children with difficulties, I decided to completely change direction and become a wedding hair stylist, and then teach hair and beauty, before finding my calling as a psychic medium, Reiki Master teacher, and spiritual mentor.

They all sound so random, right!? But I've realised that my three main careers have solidified helping people to become the truest version of themselves in mind (counselling), body (hair and beauty), and soul. Hindsight is a wonderful thing – when you can look back and realise everything you have done has been part of a bigger picture. It's fascinating to find the common thread, especially if you are a 'Jack of all trades' like myself.

This year, I will have had a business for seven years. And there are a few things that I've learnt along the way as a more sensitive business owner.

Be yourself

It's so wonderful to want to learn from others and be inspired by them. To watch their journeys and feel you would like to create something similar for yourself. It can be so easy for us to then try to be a carbon copy of that person. Or to see a particular sales strategy is working and try it for yourself. Or to watch a certain business model explode and want in on some of the action.

Of course, it's wonderful to feel inspired and we all tend to look to one another. We can't help but be influenced when we have so much we can access at our fingertips. But nothing will replace your intuition in business, and the passion you feel when something is aligned to your cause.

That expression 'people buy from people' may be a cliché, but it is true. People who are passionate about what they're doing and feel aligned to it, bring with them an energy that can't be matched, because it's congruent and our soul recognises the honesty and realness in theirs. If you are always trying to copy something someone else has already done, your soul can equally feel this, and it just won't have the same love and enthusiasm behind it.

There can be a lot of pressure and noise, especially in the online space, to do things a certain way and reach certain financial goals etc. You'll always find a guru shouting that their method can make you £5 million in five hours, and how their way is the RIGHT way. Truth be told, the only way that's right for you is YOUR way. There is no one secret formula for all to follow. We are all unique beings, with unique dreams and aspirations. We want to have different impacts on the world, and this requires us to take different paths.

You can seek advice to make sensible business decisions, of course, and you can take inspiration from those you look up to. But the real magic comes when you can take a step back and tell the world exactly who you are, and they can take it or leave it (you can even burst into the "This Is Me" song to really get your point across).

I tried for a while to use the top business coaches' strategies and systems, but I never really 'felt' it, and it always seemed false to me. I wasn't showing the 'me' in my business. I also found myself struggling with my own fears of being truly seen for who I was. I had spent so long hiding behind a carefully constructed mask, showing only glimpses of me without revealing all. I see this so often in the women I work with.

I believe this fear of being 'seen' for who you really are and the fear of 'standing out' stems from the 'witch wound' we carry from our ancestors. Years ago, especially as women, we were hunted, tortured, and slain for being different. We were called witches and burned at the stake. These survival instincts of staying small and remaining hidden are brought about by the fear instilled within us. It kept us safe for hundreds of years, and thank goodness it did.

But there are no witch hunters now, and we need to look inwards to show ourselves the love and healing needed to set aside the witch wound. Now is the time that as women, we have a voice and we are able to rise up and be ourselves, unlike our ancestors. Now, we can embrace and celebrate our differences and know it's these differences that make us the beautiful and unique beings we are.

There may be trolls and people that don't agree with you. In fact, there will be. And it isn't your job to try to convince them otherwise or try to find a version of you that they do like or accept. It's your job to allow yourself to let go of those people (and trust me, as an empath and long-term people-pleaser, I know that's far easier said than done). But there's power in putting yourself out there and allowing yourself the vulnerability of potentially receiving judgement. You do not want those haters in your world, and you will attract far more of the RIGHT people with your congruent and aligned actions.

One beautiful exercise you could do to help aid you with embracing your differences is to write a list of all the things that make you, you. All those things that make you beautifully unique. Your talents and your traits, and different examples of when you've shown these. Be sure to list why these traits are so brilliant, and don't be modest here – lean into the epic energy that is you, and don't sell yourself short.

When you have your 'Amazing You' list, you can use it to see where you'll excel in business and perhaps where you don't, which could lead you to look at where you may like to outsource etc. It can be a great idea to keep this list handy and in view when working, especially on something difficult. Keep yourself motivated by reminding yourself of the brilliant being you are.

Be open

The world is vast and there are a multitude of possibilities out there. Often in business, there can be rigidity and so much structure that you shut yourself off from certain possibilities and opportunities. Planning is important (for some more than others), but there is also a need for flexibility. If you have your whole year planned out, you cannot consider the new people and experiences you'll meet along the way. What happens if your gut is pulling you in another direction? Do you have the courage to step away from the 'plan'? Or would you view that as 'foolish'?

Truth be told, there is no right or wrong. There is no way of knowing if this new opportunity or your planned one would work better, but what I can say is that I've never experienced anyone saying that their intuition led them down the wrong path. Sure, things may not work out as you had expected, but there will always be a reason that you will later discover. Just think back over your life to something that was hard to deal with at the time, or where things didn't go according to plan – did it all work out okay in the end? Did it lead to other opportunities that led you to where you are today?

Our human selves will always want the answers and want to know why something is happening. We will wish that things would 'go to plan'. But what if your plan isn't the best thing for you, but you don't know it? What if the sequence of events about to happen will lead you to a place far beyond what you could have wished for?

This is why it is so important to be open to new opportunities and new possibilities. To allow ourselves the freedom of living in the here and now, rather than always focusing so heavily on the future and 'the plan'. I'm not suggesting that you don't have goals, I'm just suggesting a more flexible approach to them. More of a rough guideline of what you'd like, rather than something set in stone. Because, as they say, hindsight is a wonderful thing, and it's only when you reflect that you'll see the bigger picture.

It can be equally important to be open to all the messages we are receiving from our body and our soul as we are to the messages and signs from the Universe. I've found that our intuition works in the most basic of ways. It may be a divine message, but that doesn't mean it has to be complicated. One of the biggest lessons I've learnt about listening to your body and soul is that it's just as important to rest and play as it is to work.

As entrepreneurs, we tend to find it difficult to switch off. It's a sign of your beautiful passion for what you do, but it isn't the healthiest of things for your personal life (or health, at times). We can sometimes have issues with boundaries – not working past certain times or during holidays etc.

If you can feel within your body that you need to rest, then rest.

If you can feel within your soul that you need to have an adventure,

go – and have a great time.

Going against these feelings just allows the energy to build within our chakras, and they can become imbalanced or blocked. This can manifest with physical aches and pains or cause our behaviour to change. Each of our chakras are energy centres, responsible for certain emotions and responses, so when they become imbalanced or blocked, it can have a knock-on effect within our bodies.

For example, let's say your boundaries aren't too strong and you feel the need to reply to your clients as soon as you receive their messages. This may lead to an energy shift within you. It may trigger a memory of when you haven't spoken your truth or been true or kind to yourself in the past and bring forward a trauma linked with this.

This is your soul's way of warning you not to make the same mistake. You'll find your intuition telling you to leave the message – you're not working now and it's okay for the client to wait a little while. If you choose to ignore this, you're sending your soul an even stronger message that you need more help with your boundaries. You may then find yourself having a sore or tight throat, getting a throat infection/cold, or the need to keep clearing your throat.

Your body and soul are screaming to you that your throat chakra is falling out of alignment, and you need to investigate! This cycle is likely to continue until you resolve the issue and listen to the message you are receiving.

You'll likely be surprised how productive a break can be – whether for rest or to have fun! When we listen to our body and soul and work with it, rather than against it, it can work wonders for our business! It feels 'wrong' sometimes to step away from the workload, but we can come back with such vigour and passion, bursting at the seams with ideas and new creations. You went into business to be your own boss and work the way YOU want to work, so do that, and allow yourself some rest and some playtime in the process.

If you would like to clear your energy centres yourself to rebalance your chakras, you can complete a simple exercise:

1) Close your eyes and take a few deep breaths.

2) Ask your spirit guides to step forward and help you (you don't need to have met them before, they are always with you, guiding you).

3) Set the intention that you would like to clear any stagnant energy within your chakras and be given any messages of support in doing so.

4) Hold your hand on or over each of the seven main chakras, starting from the root chakra, and breathe into that space, clearing any old energy,

and sending love and healing to that area. Every time you inhale, you are sending love and healing to that area. Every time you exhale, you are releasing any old energy.

5) Repeat this for all seven main chakras. They are located along the centre of your body:

- Root – The base of your spine

- Sacral – Your lower belly

- Solar Plexus – Just above your belly button

- Heart – Your chest

- Throat

- Third Eye – In between your eyebrows

- Crown – Very top of your head

As you complete this exercise, just notice anything that comes up for you. You may see, hear, smell, taste, feel (physical or emotional), or know things. There is no right or wrong – just notice.

You'll NEVER feel ready

We all seem to be under this same delusion when we start a business (or do anything in life, really) that there will come a point in time that we will feel 'ready' to do something scary or out of our comfort zone. Almost as though someone will come along and give us the nod of approval that now is the time. Unfortunately, that isn't true.

We are taught by society that someone will either give us a congratulatory pat on the back or let us know we need to start again. At school, we have the teachers, and at work, we have our bosses. So, it's natural that becoming your own boss can present some problems with not knowing whether something is 'good enough' or whether you're 'ready'.

This continues throughout your business life. Every time you put a new offering into the world, you'll wonder whether it's good enough or if anyone will like it. Imposter syndrome will come out in full force. Your human brain will make you question yourself – as a defence mechanism, to keep you safe, within your comfort zone – working similarly to the 'witch wound'.

If you wait until the day you 'feel ready' to get started, you will never start! You can dress up procrastination as 'thorough planning', but your business and your creations will never be 'perfect'. There may be spelling mistakes, there may be a tech issue, there may be slight issues with the messaging – all these things are better than your creation not existing at all. Your creation being out in the world, imperfect, far outweighs it sitting on your computer or in your mind – perfect.

There will always be more qualifications you could gain, or more knowledge you could absorb. There will always be someone else with more experience or who you perceive to be better at what you do than you. Your human brain will ALWAYS come up with some reason why you 'should' stay exactly where you are right now. It's safe, it's the known. It doesn't require any risks to stay still.

But in the famous words of Henry Ford: *"If you always do what you always did, then you'll always get what you've always got."* So, if you have dreams and a vision for yourself and for your business, but it isn't there yet, the only way to get there is to try something new and take the risk to step outside your comfort zone.

Today, take this as your sign to take that risk in your business. Whether that means starting it or putting a new offer out there – you'll never know until you try. If you can feel that fire in your belly about the impact you're going to have on the world, go for it. If you can feel your intuition telling you that this is the right and next move for you, no matter how scary – go for it.

Ask yourself the famous question that Dr Pepper brought us – what's the worst that could happen? Sure, you could remain walking as you are comfortably, but what if this new creation helps you to soar?

Believe in yourself and your mission. You will make mistakes along the way because we all do – we are human! And in making those mistakes, this is your proof that you are trying. If you can get yourself to the place where things not going your way is a learning curve, you'll excel even faster in your business.

Being in business takes courage, and being successful in business takes resilience. You have both, otherwise you wouldn't be reading this book right now.

An exercise I find helpful when breaking past the barriers of the 'Imposter Monster' is to write yourself two lists:

1)   First list

Write down all your fears and doubts about yourself and the success of your business. Everything that is holding you back from moving forwards. Don't think about what you're writing or whether it makes sense – just get it on to the page. Allow yourself to read and feel the words on the page and notice what comes up for you.

Then burn that MOFO!

As you do, allow these words to be released and expelled into the Universe. Exhale them out of your system. And then cleanse your physical and spiritual space. You can do this through having a shower, washing your hands etc. and visualising the fears running down the drain with the water.

2)   Second list

Write ALL your achievements – big and small, personal and business/work related. Anything you're proud of – add it to the list. Highlight those things on the list that you'd consider your biggest achievements.

Keep this list in your work area, and you may like to take it with you when you are pushing yourself to step outside of your comfort zone. Read through it, feel the words on the page and allow yourself to feel the happiness and celebration to wash over you. These are your accomplishments, and they show just how incredible you are. Any time you are in doubt or don't feel 'ready', re-read this list with pride, before achieving the next goal and turning it into an accomplishment.

Life and business can be so much easier when you lean into the support you naturally have around you. Whether you choose to work with your spirit guides to receive messages of guidance, or whether you just choose to tune into your intuition, remember you are never alone. Being in business can be lonely, but when you follow your gut on the people and decisions you make, things become a lot easier.

YOU are enough, and you are perfect just the way you are.

Follow your intuition, and allow yourself the freedom of being open to the endless opportunities around you. There is no 'right way' of doing things.

You are capable of achieving anything you want in life. If you have a dream, don't allow your 'human' to dampen it. Let your soul take the lead and have fun (and rest) along the journey – it's going to be an exciting one.

LAURA CLINTON

Laura Clinton is an equine musculoskeletal therapist and founder of Equicantis, an exercise prescription app for equine and canine physical therapists.

After 12 years of treating horses and creating time consuming exercise plans that weren't user friendly for the animal owner, Laura stepped up to solve the problem. She now finds herself in the SaaS startup space as a founder of a tech product that allows fellow animal physical therapists to create digital, professional exercise plans for their clients. Laura launched Equicanits in August 2021 and has big plans to develop the platform to increasingly serve her profession.

Find out more at:

www.linktr.ee/equicantis

The Accidental Founder – I'm No Expert

Turn it off and on again, and if that doesn't work, whack it.

Up until now that has been the extent of my technical knowledge. Actually, it's not got much better. But I'm now the co-founder of a web app and find myself in the start-up SaaS space (Software as a Service, as I have learnt!) thinking about whether or not to try and pitch for investment. This was not exactly in my five-year plan (not that I even had one of those). But here I am, heading up a subscription-based app, wondering what the hell I'm doing, but successfully solving a bunch of business problems for the equine and canine physical therapy industry.

It's that latter part that I do know something about. I'm an Equine Musculoskeletal Therapist – I have qualifications in Equine Sports Massage Therapy and Equine Musculoskeletal Manipulation Therapy. Basically, I treat horses' muscles, joints and spines to help them be more balanced, straight and supple, to restore function and increase performance. And that's what I've done since qualifying in 2010.

After you've treated a horse, it's commonplace to leave an exercise or rehab plan for the owner to follow to help improve their horse's issue. So, at the end of the appointment, I show them the exercises I want them to do and watch them perform them. I'd then scribble out on paper what, how and when to do the exercises and the owner would be left with a scratty piece of paper and some verging on illegible instructions. Often, I would go back to see a client and they'd lost the piece of paper, my writing was now stained with dirt or horse poop, or I'd watch them do the exercises and think, Jesus Christ this is definitely not what I showed you. But it wasn't their fault, how could they be expected to remember?

One day I came home after treating horses, sick to death of writing out exercise plans by hand and raged about it to my husband, Dave.

I remembered seeing a human massage therapist myself a while back, and that they were using some software to send out exercises. I decided there and then that we needed to build something to solve this problem, because I knew I wasn't alone in my frustrations. I knew there must be a better way that would help fellow professionals in my industry and ultimately, help the horse. I say 'we' because I should probably mention that Dave is a web and software developer...

This must have been 2018, and I can't remember whether this conversation happened before or after we'd had our first child, Joshua. Baby brain is 100% a real thing! He was born in the July, and I was back treating horses part time three months later. It was a period of change for many reasons, entering motherhood of course, and making some business and work-life balance decisions.

I have a background in journalism and PR with a degree in Journalism, Film and Broadcasting from Cardiff University, followed by a few years spent writing for newspapers for the Midlands News Association, gaining my senior reporter NVQs.

After that, I decided to take some time out and went travelling to South America for two months, which is undoubtedly the best thing I've ever done. I came back and juggled shovelling shit at a racing yard and working with my parents in their successful catering business. I did shower in between the jobs, I promise! I then got a job in what we journalists at the time called 'the dark side' or 'selling our souls' – PR. I worked for a not-for-profit that supported local food and drink producers and retailers, so I don't think too much of my soul was sold.

Back to 2018, and Dave had been saying for a while that we should combine our skills and work together, but I'd moved on from that career and was happy with my work treating horses. This changed a bit after having Joshua and it felt like a good time to explore that, so I started to split my time between treating horses and being in the office trying to figure out what my role there was. The idea was to bring some PR and copywriting services into Dave's business, Titan Webtech, but it just never really felt right. To be honest, I think I was suffering with a lack of confidence in myself and my abilities. In the background I had been doing research on how we could solve this equine exercise prescription problem but hadn't made any moves on it, it was still just an idea. But when the PR and copywriting services just weren't aligning for me, I started to talk to Dave more seriously about building what is now Equicantis.

Lots of research, some potential audience figures, some potential financial figures, and Dave and I decided to start creating it. Like I said, I'm not techy and I don't understand the first thing about building a software product, so it has been a huge learning curve! It started off with lots of pieces of A4 paper with biro drawings of page layouts and functionality. I'd hand them to Dave saying 'like this' and he'd say 'okaaaaay' with a perplexed expression on his face. And that's how we rolled! I'm not sure I was his ideal client!

Fast forward to 2020 and development had gained momentum. I was working part-time treating horses and part-time on Equicantis; filming and building the exercise library, project managing and steering the features and design, testing, continuing to suss out our market and build connections and learning a whole heap of stuff along the way. I had planned to launch by the end of 2020 but one thing I have definitely learnt is that things take way longer than I think.

My appreciation of web and software development has skyrocketed. I have learnt that 'can you just' is NOT a phrase in development. I was also going to launch with just an equine exercise library and phase in a canine exercise library, but I decided to create and launch them both together. So, we ended up launching at the end of August 2021. There may have been some kind of pandemic happening in the background during that 12–18 month period, as well as being pregnant and having our second baby, Harrison, a few months earlier in March 2021.

I thought my first maternity leave was pretty short but this one was fairly non-existent. However, I will be forever grateful that Harrison was the best baby that you could ever wish for. Some universal powers must have been at play or I might still be trying to launch!

Phew, hooray, we've launched! Now what?

Equicantis hit the market as an equine and canine exercise prescription app for animal physical therapists. Think physiotherapists, sports massage therapists, chiropractors, osteopaths etc. They subscribe to Equicantis on a monthly or annual basis to create digital, bespoke exercise plans to send to their clients i.e., the horse or dog owner. Pressing the 'go live' button actually felt like an anti-climax. I did feel relief. I did do a little happy dance. But I also felt anxious. The moment just didn't seem to do justice to the stress, the tears and the mixed emotions of barely any maternity time. Not to mention the struggles of not knowing what the hell I was doing and if I should even be doing it. But also, to the excitement and pride of what we'd accomplished in having just launched a SaaS product and the massive amount I'd learnt. A weird set of thoughts and emotions.

I think it felt like an anti-climax because it was the realisation that there was now a different set of challenges to face. I now had to sell it. I had to make this all worth it.

At the time of writing, it's 18 months since the launch of Equicantis and it's been a real labour of love. Is it where I want it to be? Nope. Am I where I want to be? Nope. But that's ok. I have such an eagerness to create more features and continue to help my fellow practitioners that it can often leave me tied up in knots. I'm so busy looking at what I haven't done yet that I forget to pause and look at how far I have come. Giving myself credit is not something I find it easy to do. I will however, always cheer other people on and recognise their achievements. But I have come a bloody long way and I am proud of what I've achieved so far. There. I said it.

Here are some of the biggest lessons I've learnt along the way:

1.   The mindset bollocks really isn't bollocks!

I was introduced to mindset work about 10 years ago when I entered the world of network marketing with a company called Forever Living. I was part of that company for about five years, and although in the end I decided it wasn't a long-term path for me, it taught me an awful lot. I thought 'working on your mindset' and 'personal development' was a whole load of hippy bollocks, but it was a fundamental part of Forever. This meant I read and listened to a lot of interesting and inspiring people. I delved into some science and it also opened up my mind to the power of energy and the universe. Needless to say, I'm now fully on board with 'the hippy bollocks'.

As a sidenote, through building a business within Forever, I did learn a few things about how to and how not to connect with people, different ways to sell and offer opportunities, and what I was and wasn't comfortable with. I learnt a lot about people, it was very eye opening, and about getting out of my comfort zone. But I have also since discovered that there is a difference between getting out of your comfort zone and listening to yourself with what sits right and what doesn't. I sent some messages that were definitely very cringe, because I didn't listen to myself. But I met so many wonderful, inspiring people and I do have some regrets about how I left behind some of those friendships when I decided to step away from Forever. I do however believe that sometimes people are meant to be in your life for periods of time and for certain reasons, perhaps unbeknown to both parties at the time.

After having both my boys I was left with a bit of an identity crisis, which I know is not uncommon for new mums. With Joshua it led to me making some changes and joining Dave's business. But with Harrison it was much deeper, I think because I was pulling myself in too many directions at once and was playing out a narrative of 'shoulds'. As we were in the final stages of finishing and launching Equicantis when Harrison was born, I felt like I didn't have the space to be a mum, nor was I able to give what I felt was required to Equicantis. It made me ask a lot of questions about society, the roles of women, what were my truly independent choices versus what I was doing because I felt it was expected within society. That could be a whole other chapter! I was feeling pretty lost, but I didn't fully recognise it at the time.

In October 2021 a sponsored post landed in my Facebook feed from a woman called Andrea Callanan offering a free five-day online masterclass called 'Get Out of Your Own Way.' I see a lot of challenges pop up but this one really spoke to me. There was something about Andrea that felt so genuine that I just knew it was something I had to do. It was a real eye opening few days and off the back of it, I did something that I've never done before… I signed up to her group coaching course 'Unapologetic Self Mastery'. It was a lot of money for me. I discussed it with Dave and explained how I had been feeling, and I was really grateful for his support. It was bizarre to spend so much time and money learning and investing in myself. I hadn't realised the scale of my self-sabotage and imposter syndrome. But what was really enlightening was that I wasn't alone! Mindset will always be a work in progress, and self-development will be ongoing, but I've certainly learnt just how important it is.

Meeting Andrea and enrolling on Self Mastery helped me no end in navigating my way through my different roles in life. I want to have achieved everything yesterday and I get frustrated with things I feel I lack to do that, which can keep me stuck. Apparently, it's also part of an over-achiever's mindset, which is something I never would have said about myself. It's why I'm always late – because I want to do 'just one more thing' before I leave. So, there you go friends, I'm not a lousy time-keeper, I'm an over-achiever, haha!

But I do put a lot of pressure on myself to be, and do, all the things. This can leave me with a constant feeling of failure and not being good enough, because after all, who the hell am I to be running a SaaS business? I often allow myself to get plagued by a long list of 'shoulds' – I should have achieved this, I should be able to do this, I should have done things differently, I should know, I should be braver, smarter, better etc. During Self Mastery my group coach was the wonderful Beck Harrison, she recognised this trait and banned me from using the word 'should' – it's tricky, though!

Thankfully, I can recognise a lot of these undesirable patterns when they creep in now, understand where they stem from, and have a bunch of mindset tools to reset myself. But like I said, work in progress!

2.   Let go of the expert status

I've always had an issue with being an 'expert'. If you're an expert in your field, that's great. But what does the term really mean? What makes you an expert over someone else? In terms of marketing, 'position yourself as an expert' is understandable, so people will trust you. But what if you're not an expert in a particular thing? Does that mean you're doomed to a life of inadequacy, unfulfilled dreams and an empty bank balance? NO!

But I did think that this was the case up until quite recently. And it's something I do still battle with. I've never considered myself an expert in any one thing, I've always told myself that I'm average at lots of different things and believed that to be successful (whatever that means to you), you have to be an expert. You have to be at the top of your field, the best, like you can only have a handful of experts in any one area. This mentality has kept me stuck. I think it's also why I've chopped and changed what I've done as a career, to try and find that 'thing' that I'm really good at. Don't get me wrong, I believe I'm a great equine musculoskeletal therapist, but there will always be people with more extensive qualifications and experience, you can say that for everything. But I am an expert at being me and bring my own unique skillset to everything I do. Everyone can say that. I just think the word and meaning of 'expert' is overrated and overused.

A huge shift moment for me was discovering something called Human Design. If you've never looked into it, do! You can get free charts all over the place but get a session with someone who knows how to read it properly, it's very different from a personality test. Sharonah Luderitz was another person I met through Self Mastery and listening to her interpret my Human Design was like being given permission to just be me! There were so many lightbulbs but the main one was that I'm classed as a multi-passionate, so my very being is not designed to stick to one thing. And this is the thing I've always held in such high regard, that you should be an expert! It blew my mind. But it made sense to me straight away. I have so many things I'm interested in and would love to know more about and pursue, but I have to rein myself in and focus on where my time and energy has to go in the present.

I learnt that some of my strengths in relation to business are ideas and creation, and I need the right people around me with other skillsets to carry those ideas forward so I can start the creative process again. Which I do find hilarious because I've always said that I'm not creative because I'm a bit crap at art and craft! But the more I think about it, I am actually pretty good at coming up with ideas within the businesses I'm involved in, and this does take the pressure off thinking I 'should' do everything myself.

Not long after this, a colleague said to me:

"You know the phrase, Jack of all trades, master of none?"

Me: "Yeah, it's plagued my life."

"Did you know that's not the entire phrase, there's another half?"

Me: "Er no, go on…"

"Jack of all trades, master of none, is oftentimes better than master of one."

SHUT UP!

A phrase that I have been so hung up on is actual bollocks! Isn't it crazy how language and phrases change over time along with the meanings we associate with them.

This obviously isn't a dig at people who are an expert, I think if you're an expert in your field, that's brilliant! It's more of a shove into the light for those of us who aren't, or who don't desire to be, because that's just not who we are. Those of us who are multi-passionate, multi-skilled generalists, not specialists. With a little knowledge about a lot of things. Or a lot of knowledge in one thing, but also have a number of different interests to explore. It is NOT a negative thing! We need to just keep doing what we love, follow our gut and follow paths that allow our multi-faceted selves to shine.

3.   Admit when you need help (I'm trying!)

I can be afraid to ask for help because I feel I 'should' (sorry, Beck) be able to do everything myself. (Apart from accounts and bookkeeping, very open with admitting that is not a strength!) Asking for help is something I know I need to do more of and realise that it's not a sign of weakness, in business and in life. I also don't want to put on people. But no one can do everything. We all need people around us to help and support us. I am starting to outsource a few things but find it tricky to get the balance, particularly with being a start-up. I also have to appreciate and get the balance right with being a mum of two young boys.

I'm trying to learn more generally about business and entrepreneurship, and coming to terms with saying that I'm an 'entrepreneur'. I've never felt comfortable with it, like I don't deserve it, but that is what I am. So I need to start stepping into that and owning it. Hi, I'm Laura and I'm an entrepreneur.

I'm currently looking into whether pitching for investment is a route I want to go down to help grow the business and help more people with what Equicantis offers. I feel very out of my depth with it all, it feels very Dragon's Den. But what is really interesting is that since starting to talk about this, friends and connections have popped up all over the place with help and advice, when I didn't think I had anyone to turn to. Friends I've known for years but never really talk business with, or acquaintances offering help or putting me in touch with others. Even people on social media that I'm not overly familiar with pointing me in the right direction. This is currently leading down some exciting paths to help me grow the business and myself. You never quite know where help and advice is going to come from, and then you realise there was a reason that a person had crossed your path. I'd also like to think I've been that person for others too, for one reason or another.

Joining a women's business group has also been a big game changer for me. Having a group of like-minded female entrepreneurs as a support group, in the unique environment Nicola Peake has created in Peakes Private Members Club, has been so powerful.

I've not made a decision on whether to try and pitch for investment yet, I think that is going to be a big 2023 question. But reaching out for help and support has put me on the right path to help me make that decision.

Reflecting back and focusing forward

"Well, it's alright for you, you're married to a software developer."

"Yeah I know, handy right?"

This has been the gist of a few conversations I've had.

And it's definitely a good point. But it's something I've used in a self-deprecating way for a while. True, my idea would still be an idea without Dave as the co-founder because I certainly couldn't afford to pay a team of developers to build my idea for me. And that's probably why it hasn't been done like this before. I think it's amazing that our unique set of circumstances and skills has meant that we have been able to solve a problem for so many people.

Dave has always wanted to create his own marketable piece of software or application, so me bringing a concept, different knowledge base and varied skillset has also scratched an itch for him in a different way. We're both the types of people who look for opportunities. So the point here is about looking for opportunities, building relationships (you don't have to marry them all) and seeing what you can create within your own circumstances. Equicantis is still driven by a lot of our sweat equity. We put a lot more time and effort in than we take out financially. We plough the vast majority of the profits back into the business to aid its growth. It can be a bitter pill to swallow sometimes, but I'm in this for the long game. Equicantis is already helping fellow practitioners in the equine and canine physical therapy industry, and I have a deep belief that what I have planned will make a huge impact on how practitioners manage their businesses. In return, it will change mine and my family's lives, and create a legacy for my children.

Looking back, I always thought my skills were fragmented. I was someone who just regularly pivoted on the quest to find the next thing that I could try and 'be an expert in'. But it turns out these jobs, qualifications and skills have all played a part in creating Equicantis. I still have so much to learn about business and entrepreneurship, but I am enjoying the ride! I'm learning that I really need to listen to myself more, trust my gut and my intuition and that if things don't go quite according to plan then that's ok and there's a lesson there. I've discovered that asking for help isn't a sign of weakness. I am not someone who has 'made it', far from it, but that's the reason I wanted to share my story so far. I'm just someone who is taking action on an idea and figuring it out along the way. I have had so much support and advice in this business so far that I hope one day to be able to pass some words of wisdom onto others, maybe once I've figured out what the hell I'm doing! But who knows, maybe this chapter has given something to someone already. That would be wonderful.

LISA ROADS

Lisa is the Holiday Property Coach.

After investing in property since her twenties and a successful senior management career, Lisa launched her entrepreneurial journey. She founded, scaled, and transitioned two service companies that filled gaps in the holiday property market, serving hundreds of properties and guests over twenty years.

She is now focusing on her passion for business coaching. Working with Lisa within her Five P's (Property, People, Processes, Positioning, and Profit) program, she now helps holiday letting business owners scale a profitable, customer focused hosting business.

Lisa lives in Gloucestershire with her partner Clive and her rescue collie Poppy. She is passionate about travelling, photography, and interior design, drawing inspiration from her travels.

Connect with Lisa:

www.linkedin.com/in/lisaroads/

www.theholidaypropertycoach.wordpress.com

www.facebook.com/theholidaypropertycoach

www.linktr.ee/lisaroads

The Entrepreneurial Super Connector

I fit in everywhere, but belong nowhere!

This is the common thread of someone like me; a nomadic, military, boarding school child who grows up moving from place to place, boarding school to boarding school, job to job, looking for where she fits in and can eventually put down some roots and call somewhere home.

It's taken a long time to appreciate this nomadic trait and lack of roots has built the character that gave me the independence and skills to travel, explore, and spontaneously embrace opportunities that presented themselves, chat easily with strangers, and make connections. Ultimately, many of my closest multi-national friends and business networks have grown from this lifestyle.

Over the years, I have had so many random conversations with strangers, which have led me to enjoy new experiences around the world and connect with some interesting and inspiring people. From the conversation on a flight to Bangkok with the lady who was travelling as a missionary, to the six-foot bean pole American man stuck overnight at Heathrow Airport who was a specialist engineer working on submarine propellors.

I have never really seen this as a 'skill' but something that came naturally to me as someone who was curious and interested in people and people watching; how they live their lives and what they do. Being interested in people could be called being nosey, but I find people fascinating. Why do people choose (or fall) into the career they have? What do they love? What are their dreams and goals?

I have often mused that I overlooked an obvious career choice of working for MI5 or MI6 using my memory and people skills to gather intelligence!

The first school my parents chose for me was a small girls' school in Oswestry, rural Shropshire in the UK. I arrived there as a very young 11-year-old and from that day connecting with other girls at school who became my new family was what got me through my years living away from my real family.

On the plus side, it also taught me other useful skills such as how to get away with rebelliously washing my greasy hair in the dark at night, hosting fabulously creative midnight feasts, creating our own fashion catwalk parties, and playing bunk bed rounders without getting caught by pretending to be sound asleep by the time the duty matron hot-footed it up the stairs to chastise the guilty herd of elephants in the room above.

Does anyone else recall having a career interview at school?

I remember mine because it was so laughably unhelpful that it has stayed with me my whole life!

It's a great example of how to leave an impressionable student with a limiting mindset on what they might be good at or aspire to do for a career.

For a start, it was a middle-aged man which was a novelty because at our all-girls boarding school, all the teachers were women. But secondly, because he didn't leave a very positive impression on me with his less than enlightening suggestions of what my possible career options could be! He may as well have suggested I consider being a spy from the short ten-minute chat we had.

It went a bit like this!

"What subjects do you enjoy?"

"History and Geography!"

"Anything else?"

"Maybe English Literature!"

My choices of subjects were heavily influenced by my respect and appreciation of the teachers that taught these subjects and not because I was particularly good at them!

"Perhaps you should consider being a librarian or a museum curator" A what?

Now anyone who has known me even for a short while would now be laughing into their coffee reading this! Me, Lisa Roads, who would fail a sponsored silence, can't sit still, has got the patience of a gnat, sit quietly in a library or a museum?

It was never going to be a good combination and it won't surprise anyone that I didn't pursue either of them!

I passed through my education years with no clear career plan, not knowing what my 'why' might be! But with hindsight, does anyone know what that is aged 13?

Advice for that 13-year-old girl

If I were to offer career advice to my 13-year-old self, it would be to consider talking about your personality traits, social skills, and the passions you have, rather than focusing solely on academic subjects. This approach might sow the seed of something that could ignite a curious entrepreneurial mind and lead towards a more fulfilling career more quickly. There is nothing wrong with trying out jobs to find out what you do and don't like and to grow your business skills, but wouldn't it be helpful to start with something that you feel passionate about and actually look forward to going to every day?

I would have encouraged myself, rather than trying to fit in with the idea that we should all be aspiring to work for someone else; to stand out and embrace my differences and create my own career opportunities doing something I loved; and to have the courage to work for myself much earlier than I did.

But the biggest question I still ask myself is, "How did I end up here? How did I, the not particularly academically gifted, nomadic girl, end up as an entrepreneur?"

The daughter of parents that were neither academic nor entrepreneurs in my early years; nor pushy with high expectations of us apart from good manners and good people skills. But here I am, the founder and owner of not one but three successful businesses, a passport full of stamps from my many travels around the world, and a network of international friends and business associates – people I met and connected with on my travels.

My father completed 22 years in the British Army and was based all over the world during his career. Whilst he enjoyed his time in the military from the age of 16, it was only when he retired from nomadic military life and walked into the first job that he applied for that he tried working for someone else.

He soon realised that he could work hard and use his skills to make his own business a success, rather than doing that for someone else.

Aged 40, this was my father's step into the life of an entrepreneur, and he very much took the whole family along on his journey. It was a family business, and we were all expected to muck in and help. To earn my keep, my tasks were cash reconciliation and banking at the end of each day, cleaning and restocking his van every weekend and delivering emergency purchases to his customers. Whilst I wasn't always impressed at scrubbing out a dirty Snap-on Tools van at the weekend, what I did appreciate was my father's solid work ethic and commitment to building great connections with his customers, something I took away with me.

Due to my parents transitioning out of military life and into civilian life, I fell through the gaps of eligibility for local funding. So, unable to take my place at university, I took a different career path, I call it the University of Working Life path!

Be like 'Mr Ben' and try lots of careers

At the age of 20, and on the advice of my entrepreneurial father, I ventured into my first property investment, a terraced miners' cottage in Tyne and Wear, miles away from where I lived with my parents in Suffolk. It stretched me financially and I had no clue what I was doing, but I did it anyway. Determined to make my investment work (in the days before the internet), I had to work very much on the hoof to find out what I needed to know about setting up my short term let and make it work.

My career path started as a civil servant working for the Ministry of Defence in varying interesting roles, which later created the opportunity to live in Saudi Arabia, working for the Foreign Office in export to the Middle East. This role gave me a high-level insight into the importance of international working relationships for the success of international joint ventures and business collaboration within the largest companies operating in the aerospace and pharmaceutical sectors, Rolls Royce, BAE Systems and Johnson & Johnson to name a few.

My three years living and working in such a culturally different country were both enlightening and a real stretch for my personal growth, being right at the front of international trade and industry taught me so many things about how big business is done. There is a lot of building trust and relations, then there were always the social events which cemented the business relationships.

The only conscious decision I made after my time living in Saudi Arabia was that I wanted to experience working in the private sector, and that led me into the Bio-Medical and Technology sectors in roles developing commercially strategic collaboration partnerships with companies all around the world. At the start of the first role, I felt totally out of my depth. The company was not clear on what they wanted me to achieve for them and I was the only female senior manager in a large team of male technical engineers.

Undeterred, I knew that connecting people was my superpower and it played to my strengths!

I proved that I was good at building commercially beneficial relationships and in doing so, enabled companies to win higher value, more complex contracts; boosting their skills and competencies, their resourcing and their capability to deliver contracts that would otherwise have been impossible for them to deliver on their own.

However, in business things don't always go to plan even when you think things are going well! Be prepared for unexpected curve balls!

My unexpected curve ball arrived in the form of redundancy!

So, what does an experience like redundancy teach us about ourselves?

What does any business failure teach us, because they are going to happen!

What it taught me was: it's not personal, it's business.

Secondly, it's not fun but it was the catalyst that got me motivated enough to decide now was the time to start my own business so I had control over my own destiny, including when, how and who I worked with.

Any personal or business failure is an opportunity to learn and grow, providing us with knowledge, experience, and a few ego dents on the way.

Imperfect action is better than no action

From this, I knew it was time to stop procrastinating and get on with being self-employed! But it was a big, scary, overwhelming next step. I had limiting beliefs that you couldn't be a company director unless you had a business degree or a degree at all. How would I, without O Level Maths, operate business accounts? So many questions and so many limiting reasons that I could have listened to and not moved forward.

My first business in 2002 was a partnership with a great friend and work colleague. We worked together in a technology company, and for differing reasons, we felt it was time to leave and start our own businesses. We set up a company offering outsourced marketing services to SME technology companies. We leveraged my great network of business referral partners, and we already had a hit list of smaller technology companies we knew needed our help.

These two factors enabled us to quite literally hit the ground running – in heels! I will always recall the occasion when Michelle managed to snap one of the heels of her beautiful court shoes right before we were about to pitch to a company. Forever the professionals, we stuck it on in true 'Blue Peter' style and she did the pitch – remembering not to move around too much while she presented!

With a broken shoe heel, we won another contract, which really does demonstrate the point of imperfection action! This business grew quickly thanks to our complementary business skills; and for the skills we didn't have in-house, we formed strong partnerships with copywriters, design studios and web designers to enable us to offer a full agency service to our 20 clients.

In 2004, I diversified and picked up on my property investment interests, something that I had started in my early 20s. This time, I went further afield to Cyprus, to invest in two off-plan properties. At this stage, I had no clue that this event alone would lead me to my next big business opportunity. A year later my properties were completed and like any other owner, I had to get my property styled, furnished and up and rented quickly to wash its face and cover the mortgage!

Landing in Cyprus to naively undertake this task in a week, I very quickly learnt that Cyprus was years behind the UK when it came to choice of basic shops, let alone large home department stores or an IKEA – the holy grail for most investment property owners. It took me many wasted miles to stressfully pull together a cohesive Mediterranean scheme with furniture available within a few weeks. I left with an incomplete property, had to quickly appoint one of a very few property management companies to key hold for me and couldn't get my property up and rented for several months.

When I returned to the UK I was approached by other property investors who had purchased on the same development as I had, who began asking me how I had completed the furnishing of my properties and who I had appointed to manage them. My light bulb entrepreneurial moment was that this service would be in demand by investor owners just like me and I knew exactly what they needed.

While still working in my other marketing business in the UK, I started to create my next business, The Investor Complete Service, and positioned this "done for you" service to the other investor owners I knew on my complex. Knowing it would be more cost-effective to have someone do it for them, they all said, "yes, please!"

I started by creating the inventory they would need. Then I reached out to some larger furniture suppliers in Cyprus to form a working partnership for them to source and supply the bulk of the inventory. For the items which created the unique colour-styled scheme, I purchased soft furnishing and accessories in the UK and bulk shipped them to Cyprus. I would then arrive in Cyprus, clear my shipments through customs at Limassol port – a unique experience as this was something women generally didn't do at the time. Over two weeks, I would employ local tradespeople and support teams and project manage the installation of up to 25 properties at a time. From beds and sofas to soft furnishings, and air conditioning units to light bulbs and teaspoons, by the time we finished the beds were made, the properties were cleaned, and the professional marketing photos were taken.

Over the next three years, the property investment market in Cyprus snowballed and so did the growth of my business, which I continued to manage from the UK. I recognised the next critical service investment owners needed was a professional property management and rental marketing service to make their investments really work for them. So, I expanded my service offering to include these services. I did this initially using contractor team members so that I didn't have to risk carrying huge staff overhead costs and could flex my resourcing up and down to manage the level of service we would have to deliver across the different rental seasons.

I grew the property inventory of holiday rentals we managed from a few up to several hundred over the next five years. We expanded the geography we could cover and recruited satellite teams of local managers and tradespeople to provide housekeeping, cleaning, garden and pool maintenance, plumbing, and electrician services. I couldn't have increased my service reach across a large island without the initial collaboration relationships I had in place, who I could back off the local services to, until such time as I had the economies of scale and the revenue to directly employ my own team.

Things never run smoothly in business and certainly not in the hospitality sector managing guests arriving all days of the week and at all times of the day and night! The lessons I learnt about the importance of proactive preventative property management, strong systems and processes, and being able to call upon skilled professional people being the foundation to the success or failure of my business delivery, were integral to our successful business brand and reputation. Many local competitors didn't take us seriously because I operated below the radar, and I was not a permanent resident on the island. Instead, they focused their competitive battles against other companies, something I was grateful to avoid so I could get on with growing my business and supporting our happy customers.

Running a business remotely in another country presented many challenges and many possible points of failure. The biggest of these were people and suppliers. My advice is that relationships are the highest form of business currency. In the words of a business leader whom I have always admired, Richard Branson, "Take care of your employees and they'll take care of your business."

Wrongly selecting or mismanaging partnerships, people and contractors, would result in a knock-on impact on the business, including poor service, unhappy guests and bad reviews, all damaging the brand that I had worked really hard to grow. Instead, investing the time to select the best people and partnerships, to build trust and solid relationships, and always paying my contractors within a few days of receiving their invoices reaped its rewards. I gained a team of people I could rely on and call upon in an emergency and who would always go the extra mile to help. Commercially, I learnt to work with people with aligned values, complementing skills and always within commercial service level agreements which mirrored what we needed to deliver to our customers and holiday guests. This was the solid foundation which enabled me to scale and operate this business for 18 years.

It's never too late to start a new business

Brexit and the Covid Pandemic were the catalysts for me deciding it was time to rehome this business in 2021 to a new owner resident on the island. I was fortunate to find the new owner in a very loyal team member who not only knew the business inside out but who knew our customers and what our brand represented on the island. This made the transition and my exit so much easier, and it fills my heart to know the business and our loyal client relationships continue to thrive.

I took a year out to invest in my own personal development and restock my UK business connections, with a view to using my 18 years of holiday rental experience and launching an online business coaching other hospitality business owners to be successful. The online business space was a totally new arena for me, and I knew I needed to identify and connect with like-minded entrepreneurs who would not only support me with the skills I lacked but would give me a new business space in which to safely grow my new venture.

I looked at joining a number of business networking groups, but many of them felt very stale and traditional in their approach to networking. From early morning breakfast meetings in hotels, not great for a non-morning, non-traditional person, to all the other well-established business networking groups which required regular meeting points in dull hotels, sitting around tables with no real depth of getting to know each other.

Then one of my clients and one of my business connections both mentioned a new group called Peakes VIP Club, a new membership for entrepreneurial women who were looking for a different way to connect. This group of women connect by sharing amazing social events like spa days (I'm sold already) to business mastermind days and fun events trying something new which might take you out of your comfort zone (Wim Hoff cold water swimming springs to mind). This connection lounge attracted me because it was different, and I am different. I have found a new place to fit in and call my business home while I establish my third business, The Holiday Property Coach.

Appreciate where you started but keep moving forward

Looking back, I realise I wasted many years being unfulfilled and working hard to make other people's businesses successful. I wasted time waiting for the timing to be right to start my own business, citing my location or my age, or my lack of self-belief as reasons to delay doing it. There will never be a perfect time!

It took redundancy followed by a boss that I could not respect to be the catalyst to make me get on and do it. I haven't looked back since and that was 18 years ago.

From those first tentative steps into my first business, I have grown enormously as a person and an entrepreneur, in business and people management skills, connections and experience. I haven't looked back with any regret for finding the courage to believe that I could do it, but I didn't do it alone. I achieved it with the support and encouragement of many wonderful people whom I am very grateful to have met on this journey and I am happy to say many of whom are still with me.

Don't be afraid to be different! Entrepreneurs by their very nature tend not to fit into the 'normal mould' and this makes them innovative in business. I now know that my strength of character, my independence, and my ability to stand on my own, to make my own decisions and mistakes are also the reasons why my differences have become my strengths in business. My ability to pivot and form strong collaborations has really helped my businesses to scale over the years.

I am still inspired every day by the people I meet. Whether waiting for a train or standing in a supermarket queue, I talk to people, and have gained a reputation for being a connector and collector of people! I have uncovered some of my best business collaboration opportunities and made some of my closest friends in the most random situations. If I could pass on one piece of advice it would be to talk to people, it's how you stumble across skills and collaboration opportunities you would otherwise have missed out on.

NICKY MARSHALL

At 40, Nicky suffered and recovered from a disabling stroke – inspiring a life's mission to make a bigger difference.

Nicky has an accountancy background, 20 years of experience helping people improve their health and wellbeing, and a decade in publishing.

Nicky is a mentor, seasoned workplace facilitator and keynote speaker, inspiring people to discover their own brand of Bounce! Nicky's knowledge, knack for stressbusting, hugs, and infectious laugh make her an in demand and popular speaker.

As editor-in-chief and mentor at Discover Your Bounce Publishing, Nicky loves helping authors to find their voice and get published.

Be careful if you stand too close – her enthusiasm rubs off!

Find out more at:

www.sleek.bio/nickymarshall and www.discoveryourbounce.com

Expand Your Life, Expand Your Business!

They say hindsight is a wonderful thing, but wouldn't it be great to know all of this hindsight-ed goodliness before you start? Or at least before you give up.

I've been in business in various forms for 16 years now and I can't tell you the amount of times I've threatened myself with working in Tesco to have an easier life...as a qualified accountant I'm not sure why Tesco, perhaps it's my dramatic nature in full flow when I'm frustrated!

My work history starts with 10 years in finance before, with a one year old and a three year old, I decided to re-train as an accountant. If I'd had the right role models at school I'm sure this was the career I would have really wanted, but working in a bank seemed like the safer option, I suppose. Eight years of study, 21 exams and a whole lot of juggling led to the job of my dreams, the corner office, and a feeling of accomplishment. This quickly turned into a feeling of being terrified that someone would 'find me out' as the imposter syndrome kicked in, followed by endless stress, bullying, and the constant juggle of a new big, scary job and newly single mum-hood!

Somehow, I caged the beast. I got a handle on the job and introduced some great systems that I'm still proud of today. I started to balance my life and look after myself more, I learned Reiki and Reflexology (which was a life changer for my wellbeing) and stopped the bullying by standing up for myself.

The final 'standing up' was telling the company director that I would rather shelf stack in Asda than spend one more minute in his company (another supermarket reference – interesting!).

Not the planned gentle transition into self-employment I would recommend to others, but there you are, it was my start. My business as a therapist began and I loved that I could help other people with the energy boosting therapies that had helped me. I wanted more, though. I wanted to help more people and expand my business in many different ways, like speaking and networking. I also had a dream that one day I would own a therapy centre AND a coffee shop, how cool would that be? It felt impossible, but I couldn't let it go.

I had a few barriers to overcome in those early days:

I hated speaking in public. I had only ever spoken one to one and to a few board members, so going networking where you had to speak to the room was terrifying. I could feel my heart pounding as it got to my turn and was full of admiration for those people that stood up full of ease.

I had never run a business before. Sure, I could do the accounts, but marketing? Sales? I loved the graphic stuff like logos and leaflets, and realised early on that I needed to get help from professionals for that bit. Remember this was 2006, social media was in its infancy and seemed to be for fun, not work.

I was so stressed from my exit I rebelled against working too much. I had to do the school run twice a day and spent the first few months catching up with friends, starting work later and, in reality, 'playing' at being a business owner – until I realised, I just had a hobby and ideals!

After my turbulent years of separation and divorce I had re-discovered what it was like to be happy. I got to quite like being me and I think my Reiki training had a lot to do with both. A chance meeting with my brother's friend Phil had led to a blossoming romance, as well as a new found ally on my quest to being brave. Phil had no fear, from jumping out of aeroplanes to sailing the channel, this guy had been there and done it all. He travelled the world for his job and thought nothing of standing up and giving a speech with the panache I had envied.

Whenever I said I couldn't do something he would just look at me and say, "Why not?" Much of the time I didn't really have any reason, except that I was scared. So, when I shared my dream of travelling to Sedona in Arizona, rather than laughing or putting up barriers he did the polar opposite: he helped me book my flights, took me to the airport and looked after my two girls while I was gone. The plane had engine trouble so I missed my connection and my suitcase was left with another of the shuttle guests… But no-one died and I hoped for the best, as I was reading a book called *Infinite Possibilities* by Mike Dooley that explained there were always different choices to be made.

While en route to Sedona, I attended a personal development event called *Celebrate Your Life* and enjoyed talks from a host of spiritual gurus like Wayne Dyer, Iyanla Vanzant, and Sonia Choquette. Sitting in the audience, I knew I could lead a very different life. Sedona was a magical, shamanic place and I spent time with a wonderful guide called Elizabeth. She was so kind and gentle; she saw something in me that I was still struggling to see…I could see it in her eyes.

I had discovered Paganism at 27 after a chance encounter with a psychic medium, who not only convinced me of my own abilities, but also gave me insight into my love of nature, writing by moon cycles, and my inability to feel anything in Christian churches growing up. I had studied Wicca, Druidry and Shamanism, and to this day combine elements of all three into my life. I had always struggled to ground myself and often felt dizzy and floaty.

In Sedona, I found the grounding I craved. Walking the lands, being outside most of the day and really tuning into the seasons. I have been back many times since and it always feels like coming home.

There were other perks to being Phil's girlfriend…oh, and then wife!

Phil loved to ski and couldn't wait to take me. We booked a lovely break in Sauze D'Oux just before my birthday and I couldn't wait. I imagined blue skies, beautiful views, log cabins, and roaring fires, all of which I got. I just didn't realise I would be so terrified of heights, would fall down endlessly, be in floods of tears daily, and go home with a dislocated thumb and a lung infection!

I was a broken human being, but I could see the attraction of being able to ski, I knew I wanted to go again and signed up for hypnotherapy. It turned out a ride on a red sleigh when I was eight – that I had absolutely no recollection of – had led to my being terrified.

How many times, in life and business, do we encounter something that scares us? We can avoid it and do something else…or we can work our way through that block.

The result? Fifteen years of amazing ski holidays, I have skied the women's downhill black run in Chamonix and many other beautiful runs. To prove I was 'cured' I also did a tandem paraglide from 2000 metres – I did have a few butterflies but the view was incredible! Now, I would say I'm pretty fearless!

So, what does this have to do with running a business, you may ask?

Every time I have pushed a boundary in my life, I have reaped the rewards in my business. My confidence increased, my bravery increased and more doors opened.

When I was asked to speak at the Women Economic Forum in New Delhi, would I have said no because I was afraid to travel without Phil?

There have been countless times I have been terrified of what I needed to do in business – but knowing that amazing outcomes lie just beyond your comfort zone means it's worth the stretch.

There is a link between your inner world and your outer world. If you have blocks or fears, they show up in the form of challenges in your outer world. If you are overwhelmed or low on energy, your business will be slow to compensate. Time and again I have seen this happen.

I opened my 'dream' coffee shop and holistic centre in 2010 after a series of synchronicities, and I felt like the whole thing flowed. On opening night, I was buzzing. So excited I had fulfilled the vision I had been holding for years. The next day I opened the doors and the thought dropped into my head like a stone: I had to make £2000 each month just to cover the overheads. In the next three months I worked tirelessly – I was driven and scared, working 80-90 hours per week. Twelve weeks in, after a weekend of scuba diving, I suffered a cerebral bend that caused a stroke. I lost the use of my left arm and leg, and my memory and speech were affected. It took me three years to recover and I had plenty of time to reflect on what had happened.

How could the dream turn to reality so easily and yet I couldn't sustain it once we opened? I realised I had stopped looking after myself, I stopped having fun and I tried to act how I thought successful people did: driven, hustling, crushing it.

Today, with my business partner, I run three businesses. We take lots of holidays, we have fun, and if ever we struggle, we step away and take a break. We don't hustle – we visualise and strategise. We don't crush it, we take action in line with our plans.

My holidays, my fitness, my family time…all goes into the diary as a priority.

I have a mantra: 'What is meant for me will find me.' So rather than FOMO: Fear Of Missing Out, I have JOMO: the Joy Of Missing Out. This means I don't waste energy worrying that I may miss something.

Another useful phrase I've learned is 'Just because I can, doesn't mean I should'. There are many things you can do, some are shiny objects that appeal to your inner magpie, but do they take you nearer or further away from your goal?

Today, my life has more in it: more time for me, more time to be with the people I love. Our businesses are thriving and I am the healthiest I think I have ever been. I don't have more time than anyone else – we all get the same 86,400 seconds every day. I do know that I live in a very different way today, though, and that's what I'm going to share.

Fill your cup

It can be hard to know where to start with this, especially if you feel like your life is already super busy! Start by asking yourself what you like or love. You may have forgotten what it feels like to have time to yourself, so this may be tricky.

Think about having the energy for your life as well as the energy for your business. Sometimes getting more energy happens when we rest more, but sometimes it happens from doing things you love.

As Maya Angelou said, we may not remember what someone said or did, but we will remember how they made us feel. Life is about feelings, and moments that inspire feelings, so make sure your life is full of moments that make you feel good.

This may be getting a sale, cuddling your child or zip-wiring through a rainforest…we all have the best way for us and thank heavens everyone is different!

Also think about your peace of mind and wellbeing. What do you need to keep yourself healthy and content. For some people it's more sleep and time alone, for others it's a daily gym workout and time with people.

Since suffering the stroke, I must prioritise sleep. If I get 8-9 hours sleep per night I stay mentally and physically well. My immunity is good and my mood is good too. Giving up alcohol two years ago was a game changer for me for two reasons. It helped me sleep deeply – without waking up at 2am with reflux and night sweats. It also stopped me waking up on Monday morning not wanting to work. Why would I not want to work in the businesses that I loved? Drinking, not even to excess, gave me this weird defeatist, negative attitude that felt alien to the rest of my life.

Is sleep your thing? Or is it movement? Getting outside? Nutrition and hydration? It's good to be a detective in your own life and find out what you need – be curious and open to trying new routines for a few weeks to see what works.

Play in the stretch zone

To expand your life or expand your business, you need to do things differently. Our minds may want us to stay the same, to live in our comfort zone where everything is known, but this is not going to create a better life or business. In fact, as people age, their comfort zones tend to shrink; not because of their age, but because they lose confidence. They may doubt their driving ability, worry about uncertainty when travelling to somewhere new or get anxious about becoming ill. I have seen younger people acting old and older people acting young – and doing new things and stretching boundaries seems to be a positive factor.

My dad is my hero in this regard. He has never considered slowing down, and even went roller skating on his 80th birthday. When anyone asks how he is, his standard answer is 'brilliant'. He has always looked after his health, seeking solutions to any problems rather than accepting them. At the time of writing, he is 83 and still running an engineering business full time.

Pushing boundaries, making changes and learning new things is a great way to expand, but remember to pace yourself. When we change everything all at once we slip into the panic zone and this is where your amygdala gets unhappy. The amygdala is part of our fight or flight system and is constantly looking for threats, so when your world changes too much you may find yourself having a stress response that feels uncomfortable.

Try changing one or two things at a time and give yourself time to get comfortable with the new routine. When we are constantly changing, we can suffer from 'change fatigue' where we can no longer get excited about doing something new.

Bounce back-ability

To master this is to hit ninja level in life!

What if you knew, with absolute certainty that you would be at peace no matter what the situation? If you failed, if you were ill, if you had an accident or if something totally unexpected occurred?

I heard a phrase years ago, 'People plan and God laughs.' With my Pagan beliefs I have changed it slightly to, 'People plan and the gods laugh', but you get my meaning!

Life is unpredictable. People are unpredictable. We can make all of our plans, visualise, manifest, map out our future…and then something happens to change it all.

I am reminded of March 2020!

I heard of people burning their vision boards in a temper as their plans had to change, literally overnight.

So having the ability to shift, to adapt, to embrace change and create something new is a skill indeed. When an entrepreneur is asked what they would do if their business went bust, most would reply that they would get busy doing something new.

Of course, sometimes we need time to sulk a bit or to grieve for the life we had planned. What can help this process is to practise gratitude. When we couldn't physically see our families, I was grateful that they were healthy where they were and that we had the technology to stay in touch. When I could no longer travel, I was grateful for the extra time my husband and I got to stay with each other at home. When we were allowed time to go out I was grateful for the lovely weather we had – you get the picture?

Listing your gratitudes produces serotonin in the brain that increases your happiness, but it may take some initial effort to create the habit. Try listing 10 things you are grateful for before bed and this may help you sleep deeper for longer.

The ability to bounce back can be learnt by anyone and I value it as a top life skill. It means you can burn the candle on a night out, work extra hours to deliver a project or be there to lend a hand to family and friends. You can try new things with the reassurance that if you get it wrong then you know what to do. It helps to boost your confidence, dispel your fears and create an enriched life full of memories.

In conclusion, I would like to ponder on connection and how it can reinforce your expansion in life and business.

Connect with yourself

Today's world is filled with shiny objects and can be 24/7 if you let it. There will always be a distraction, or something you 'should' do…but at least once a day connect with your inner self. Maybe place a hand on your heart and feel your breathing, or feel your feet on the ground and send your energy into the earth. Perhaps lie on the bed and let your whole body relax. Create an awareness of who you are, what you are feeling and how much energy you have.

In that moment you may realise that you are hungry, you are thirsty or you are tired. You may be happy, contented, and full of energy. When you know how you are, you know what to do next.

Connect with the planet

We live on the most amazing planet. It is beautiful, it has the ability to sustain us, and it's full of the most incredible vistas. Whether that's the view from the top of a mountain or the view from a high-rise block, I marvel at everything that has been created here. Look up, look down, look around…if you are engrossed in your list or worries you will miss the show.

Try to catch a sunrise or a sunset every day…it gives us an opportunity to think of our potential (sunrise) or give gratitude for a fulfilled day (sunset).

Be kind to animals; I avidly avoid stepping on ants or damaging plants. I say hello to trees and I'm always picking up pebbles and feathers. We're organic beings that don't do well if we're always surrounded by tech. Get outdoors, breathe it in – our planet is incredible.

Connect with people

Be present with people; smile at them, give them a compliment…you can literally change the course of someone's day. People are amazing and with the right tools and a bit of encouragement they can achieve miracles.

If someone is rude to you or unhelpful – send them love. They may be having a tough time and may deserve a break…but by getting cross you have poisoned yourself! Sending them love brings you good energy too, it's a win/win!

Connecting with people has been the number one biggest gamechanger in my business. It hasn't been the technology I've discovered or the products I've created. It's been the people I've learnt from, the people I've worked with, and the people I've had as customers.

Connect with your business

If you have a business, send it some love! Creating a business takes a huge amount of time, money, and energy, and sometimes we get setbacks. Often, we don't get the growth we expect fast enough or we can feel overwhelmed with what we need to still achieve.

Love it anyway.

Love the potential. Love the opportunity. Love this vehicle that allows you to provide a solution or a service and a financial reward for you. Love the journey, love the lessons, love it all!

Connect the dots

I believe life is constantly sending us messages, a trail of breadcrumbs that leads us to more. More happiness, more connections, more experiences, more love. When we 'get our eye in', like with those magic eye pictures that used to drive me mad, you can see the links between where we are and where we are trying to go. When we lose this vision, we get fearful, frustrated and sometimes sick...until we nudge ourselves back on track.

That said, sometimes horrible things happen to good people, and I have no explanation for that. However, if we can spend the majority of our lives trying to be kind to ourselves and others, being open to things being better, then every day we can find at least one thing to smile about.

So now it's over to you to start to expand; your life and your business. Write down your list of dreams, say yes to the 'impossible', and really feel when life starts to stretch out into the realms of infinite possibility!

RACHAEL HALL

Rachael Hall is a two-times global award winning independent financial adviser (IFA), CISI accredited financial coach and NHS pension specialist. Rachael provides holistic and bespoke advice for medical professionals, business owners and entrepreneurs. Rachael is one of the country's leading experts on the UK pension tax system. She has been featured in The Sunday Times, The Financial Times, The Telegraph and other industry news channels.

Find out more at www.linktr.ee/rachaelhall7

Disclaimer: the information contained in this chapter is meant to provide insights into financial planning for the self-employed and should not be construed as financial advice. Financial Planning should be personalised to each individual and there will be many more considerations than those addressed in this chapter alone.

Planning For Financial Freedom

It's 2003, and I'm standing in the bar of a hotel in London. The smell of stale beer fills the air, and I'm wondering whether anyone would notice if I added a shot of vodka to the Diet Coke I've just ordered - I decide against it as it'll probably just make me even more tired. My feet are aching from the new shoes I bought for the conference, and I've got a caffeine headache, having spent all day knocking back cups of coffee so I have the energy to help out at this event. Who'd have thought handing out brochures, registering people and ushering delegates into stuffy conference rooms to watch fund managers give financial presentations could be this tiring? We are now waiting for the CEO to give the final address so we can wrap up for the day.

Finally, the conference room doors open and we can hear the rumble of people leaving the room. A group of fifteen men head straight for the bar. Lumbering across the hotel lobby like a herd of geriatric elephants, they look at me and comments are exchanged which, thankfully, I can't make out. One of the men makes a beeline for me with a smirk on his face. Before I even realise what's going on, he has lifted me up and announces to the group, "I want to have sex with you!". He squeezes me hard and I feel myself turn bright red. Now I'm angry. I do not react well to humiliation.

"Sorry...I'm not into necrophilia," is my reply.

He drops me and a look of embarrassment sweeps over his chubby, reddening face, as the rest of the group of men burst into laughter. He apologises, although more to himself for his bruised ego than to me or for any sense of shame as to the inappropriateness of his actions.

This was my introduction to the world of financial services, and has no doubt acted as a springboard into a career that has been characterised by successfully challenging stereotypes to become a recognised leader in my industry.

I can thank my strong northern upbringing and matriarchal grandmother for my inner strength and resilience. It's sad to say this, but back then my 23-year-old self probably didn't think this was such a big deal, because 'pervy men' in pinstripe suits were more or less an everyday irritation that had to be dealt with in the world of financial services.

Of course, not all of the men were like that, but the patriarchy saw to it that if they were to show any degree of empathy towards a woman, that was a sign of 'weakness' and they were very much considered to be bottom of the pecking order. The odd one would roll their eyes at me in a supportive way and whisper "good on you", but only when the main offenders were no longer in earshot.

So these are the origins of the quick-talking, self-reliant and successful woman I now see when I look in the mirror, and this is the energy I have been required to develop and still carry with me. A suit of armour and a double-edged sword that has created both opportunity and isolation in equal measure. Both are still sometimes required if I am to be afforded a degree of respect from the prevailing attitudes within the industry in which I have challenged the established practice.

Fast forward 20 years from that first conference and having juggled misogyny, motherhood and inner doubt, I now have a business which is scaling. At the time of writing, Seven Medical has experienced significantly high levels of year-on-year growth, with 2022 increasing at a rate of 570% on the previous year. Most coaches would have you believe that this is living the dream, but they don't often share the ugly truths. Don't get me wrong, this can be a thoroughly rewarding period of time and I do feel proud of where I am at today – I have a national reputation as a specialist in my field, have three-month waiting lists for people wanting to join our programmes, and I feel nothing but gratitude for that level of recognition and the trust that people place in me and my team. That said, a scaling business is a fast-moving and cash hungry monster and if it doesn't get fed, this little beast will bite back with such ferocity, that it can make you question whether it's all worth it.

You may find yourself navigating burnout and experience panic attacks every time you hit new levels of income. Costs increase and as you hire more staff you will likely find yourself feeling the pressure and questioning every decision you make. Solopreneurs soon find themselves managing teams of people, a role which they never expected and for which they have no experience. Dealing with many different personality types can be overwhelming, especially if you don't hire the right people.

So if you are reading this chapter and find yourself in this position today, congratulations! You have done amazingly well to get here. Hopefully, my experiences will provide you with some insights that can help shape your journey, reduce financial turbulence, and allow you to grow in a way that both supports your mental health and wellbeing, and serves as a reminder that you are not alone!

Why do we build wealth?

"If you fail to plan, you plan to fail"

– Benjamin Franklin

According to the Association of Independent Professionals and the Self Employed (IPSE) there are 1.7 million solo self-employed women in the UK, 893,000 of whom are highly skilled freelancers. Research suggests that whilst women have high levels of job satisfaction, they find self-employment more of a challenge to navigate, with concerns around social security benefits, financial support, a lack of regular income and not being prepared for retirement; research shows that only 22% of women have any form of non-statutory pension.

Needless to say, I hate these statistics and find them particularly disempowering. There is absolutely no reason why women cannot be adept at financial planning – in my experience of death and divorce cases, many of the widows and ex-wives who did not previously make the financial decisions were much more financially savvy than their spouse and managed to create successful business operations.

So, what is the point of building wealth?

Let me answer this very simply – it gives us independence.

If you want to work for the rest of your life then great, perhaps you love what you do. But wouldn't it be preferable for that decision to be based on choice rather than necessity?

And what if the option of eternal working is taken from you due to life events, long-term illness or injury?

Do you have a Plan B?

Building wealth gives us financial security and leads to independence – success should be individually measured against individually set goals and aspirations; it is a state of mind to enable you to live your best life, free from financial anxiety.

Beginning at the end

"The trouble with not having a goal is that you can spend your life

running up and down the field and never score"

— Bill Copeland

I often find that the best place to start with your retirement or 'financial independence' plan is at the end, then you can attempt to reverse engineer your ideal outcome. It also provides a level of direction, which can be reviewed and changed annually if and when needed. Life is often unpredictable, so the journey is unlikely to form a linear pathway, with many twists and turns appearing along the way. But if we don't have something to aim for, we will spend our lives not achieving anything and being disappointed with the outcome once we reach our retirement years.

Goal setting can be a challenge. Most people don't give it any thought unless forced to do so. It's all well and good setting goals, but you also need to remember to live in between!

Ask yourself these questions:

- If I had an unlimited amount of money and were completely independent, how would I live my life?

- If I had only 5-10 years left to live, what would I change?

- If I only had 24 hours left to live, who did I not get to be?

- What's worth doing even if I fail?

- Who am I?

- Why am I doing this?

Now imagine your life as a timeline, and thinking about financial planning for the first time at 40...

Financial independence timeline

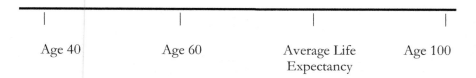

| Age 40 | Age 60 | Average Life Expectancy | Age 100 |

It can be quite depressing looking at this timeline, especially if you have done little to no financial planning. I often meet people in this position and have less than 20 years to try to help them create passive income streams which will allow them to become financially independent, or fully retire on their terms.

Ask yourself these questions:

- What duration of this timeframe do I want to spend working?

- When will the mortgage be paid off?

- What are my future income goals?

- Are there any other major events coming up that require major financial outlay and can set me back on my journey?

- Are there likely to be any financial opportunities that could bring me closer to my goals?

- When do I want to be financially independent?

Know yourself and know your numbers

One of the most commonly asked questions is, "When can I afford to retire?"

In my experience, most people seriously underestimate the complexity of this question, more so the ones who provide me with little to no information about their current finances and expect me to instantly reply with the 'magic number'.

So let's clear one thing up now: there is no universally accepted magic number. Everyone is different. Some people have a lifestyle that requires very little ongoing income, whilst others have high expectations about the independent years and require a larger degree of accessible income.

The questions you should be asking yourself are:

- How much income do I need to have a comfortable standard of living?

- What would be an aspirational level of monthly income?

- What are my current outgoings?

- Are these outgoings going to reduce or increase in the future?

In my experience, if you are unable to answer most of these questions, then it's possible that you don't understand your cashflow needs. I find the best place to start is to look over the last three to six months of bank statements to work out your average monthly income vs spending.

Assuming you don't think there are likely to be any changes to your cashflow in the foreseeable future, you can simply use this as your base level need for income purposes and continue it throughout your life span. In order to ensure these figures don't lose value, you will need to allow for future inflation and you may want to do this with the help of a financial adviser, as it can be a complex exercise.

Spending plans are another tool which can be used. So, rather than use your current income need as a *target* income, you may want to itemise your expenditure. This may include costs for activities such as holidays, hobbies, entertaining, etc., or any other activities you would like to enjoy in retirement. Don't hold back. There's no reason why you can't create an aspirational plan – every year I meet many people who believe their aspirational targets aren't achievable and we continue to prove them wrong as we retire them!

Aside from 'knowing the number', you also need to consider your own attitudes and views of money, spending and saving.

Your money mindset

Financial psychologists believe that we all have our own money scripts or narratives, which are usually half-truths or unconscious biases passed down to us from our parents and grandparents in our early childhood. These can be phrases we may have heard growing up, such as:

- "Money doesn't grow on trees."

- "There will NEVER be enough money."

- "There will ALWAYS be enough money."

- "Having more money will make things better."

- "We don't talk about money."

- "Money is the root of all evil."

According to research by Klontz et al (2011) there are four different psychological profiles:

1. **Money Avoidance** – these people repel wealth as their

unconscious belief has taken a 'vow of poverty' and as they believe there is nothing good about holding onto money, they don't ever have or talk about money. They may sabotage their own financial success and frequently give money away.

2.   **Money Worship** – they believe the key to happiness is having more and more money. They may carry credit card debt, or overspend on things, because it makes them feel better. People in this category also tend to have a lower net wealth. They tend to put work ahead of family.

3.   **Money Status** – these people often link their self-worth to their net worth. They may appear to be 'wealthy' but they are often over spenders, having come from lower socio-economic backgrounds. They may be guilty of hiding spending from their partner and prone to excessive gambling.

4.   **Money Vigilance** – the money vigilant are less likely to have debt and only spend what they can afford. They are smart savers, investors and are in good financial health. They are discreet about their financial status and rarely keep financial secrets from their partner.

Financial flashpoints

Klontz also identified that as we progress through life we may experience 'financial flashpoints' which are life-changing events that impact our relationship with money. These 'flashpoints' could represent a messy divorce, a business which goes bankrupt, even a financial windfall may impact our lives. Studies from the US suggest that over 70% of lottery winners lose all their money. They have concluded that instant changes in socio-economic status can adversely affect some people's lives, as it pushes them away from their communities, causing a decline in mental health and wellbeing. Other winners may lose the money as they have no formal financial education from which to draw. Children who grew up within families that are relatively wealthy inherit some skills and knowledge from their parents and are more likely to retain this wealth as they proceed through life.

If you have a fractured or difficult relationship with money, then you may not be able to see these plans through and no level of planning will help you, unless you first address your mindset issues.

Reviewing your existing plans

Some of you may already have invested in financial products or contribute to pensions. It is possible to request a retirement illustration from your pension company, which will give you some idea as to what your pension may be worth in the future, assuming low, medium and high rates of growth.

However (and here comes the legal bit), this is a specialist area and as a regulated financial adviser, it would be remiss of me not to warn you that these values aren't guaranteed. Investment values fluctuate and, as we say, past performance is certainly no guide to the future – I would therefore strongly recommend that you seek the help of a professional, such as a fully regulated independent financial adviser if you need to review your existing plans.

Mapping your cashflow

If we return to our timeline and add in the income streams and expenditure, it may begin to look something like this:

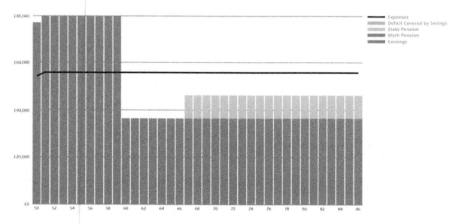

Source: FE CashCalc

As you can see from the above table, the black line is our target income level, and our expected retirement income isn't quite enough to cover this shortfall. Investing some of the surplus income during our working years, to give back to our future selves should allow us to retire either earlier than expected or on time.

Using financial products which are tax efficient, such as stocks and shares ISAs, Lifetime ISAs and pensions are also a win, as it ensures your profits are protected from different forms of taxes, such as interest, dividends and Capital Gains Tax (commonly referred to as CGT).

For the purpose of this exercise, I have assumed the client has fully exhausted pension allowances and plans to make a £20,000 yearly ISA contribution, which then covers our deficit:

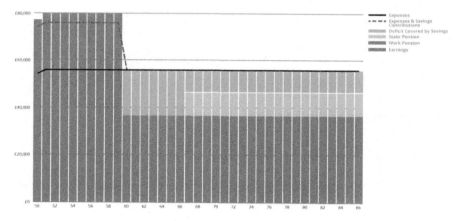

Source: FE CashCalc

Income strategies

The above graph assumes capital withdrawals will be made from the ISA, but some people may want to retain the capital and live off a percentage of profits, or choose a fixed level of income instead. Thus preserving the capital, so it can be passed down to members of the family. The frequency of the income can be planned at the outset. There has been a lot of research conducted over the years which has disputed the level of income that can be sustainably withdrawn from an investment portfolio, before running out of money. A now-retired financial adviser called Bill Bengen conducted this US-based research and concluded that an initial withdrawal of 4.5% sustained all portfolios from 1926 to 2020 (assuming tax advantaged accounts and inflation adjusted, with 30 years longevity).

So, if we apply the same ethos within this case study, it is likely that we may need to save more, adjust the level of risk or revisit our time horizons to ensure we can build enough income to hit our future targets.

The importance of reviews

Bengen was heavily critiqued by other experts. Some claimed he was too cautious, which meant people ran the risk of having too much money when they died, and didn't spend enough while they were alive. Another US based financial adviser, Michael Kitces, addressed the importance of time horizons, as not everyone needs income for 30 years exactly, and so these withdrawal rates should be adjusted accordingly.

As this is a highly complex area, it would be sensible to seek regulated financial advice. Annual reviews will ensure you remain on target and don't drift too far away from your goals. Any drift can be addressed early on and adjustments can be made to ensure you remain on track. Also remember that the figures you set yourself in the year 2023 are likely to be different in 2040. We don't know what the future holds…another pandemic, higher than expected inflation, changes in personal circumstances, fiscal policy, etc.

Reviewing your plans regularly is essential to securing the best outcome.

Protecting your plan

Once you have your design, you should protect or 'insure' it against any unforeseen events that could damage wealth and set you back to day one on your financial journey.

You can use insurance policies which pay out a lump sum (or income) if you die or suffer from a serious or critical illness or long-term illness or injury. The latter policies, known as Permanent Health Insurance (PHI) or Income Protection plans, are particularly useful for the self-employed, as they will help to remove you from the benefits system, providing a more meaningful and significantly higher level of tax-free monthly income, which can be index-linked (i.e. the benefits increase in line with inflation) and continue in payment until the day that you retire.

These policies are essential as they underpin your financial security, meaning you don't have to burn through savings or sell your house to afford to make ends meet. You can simply pick up where you left off after a temporary financial disruption, allowing you to continue your journey to financial freedom.

Collaborating with the competition

Self-development has always been really important to me. Apart from the local professional development events held by our professional membership, there were few opportunities to network with other financial advisers during the formative years of my career; especially with those from different industries, and the courses were usually only linked to a curriculum. Business courses or programmes just didn't exist.

I therefore took it upon myself to reach out to other professionals, originally seeking some form of mentorship which later became a simple form of moral support. Knowledge is the cornerstone to our clients making informed decisions. Our role in making that happen is to collaboratively upskill everyone to raise the bar generally. So, working with the competition has always been a win for everyone, in my experience.

Over the years, I have undertaken paid work for the clients of other advisers, which has helped me build more client connections through word-of-mouth referrals and given me exposure to their audience. The existing adviser was happy the client had received specialist advice and they managed to retain their relationship with the client long term, rather than losing them to another specialist.

Sometimes we worry that collaboration will undermine our futures. I'm not saying we need to adopt this as a permanent strategy, but I do think we need to be less fearful. In the early days, I always thought there were people who knew a hell of a lot more than me, having previously judged them on their successful careers, social standing and job titles. What I actually found is that many of these people seldom knew more than me in my niche area. You would be forgiven for thinking this viewpoint is being driven by my ego, but I actually think it's more complex than that, possibly a form of imposter syndrome that rears its ugly head from time to time.

Over the years, my 'competition' have become my greatest allies. We are huge supporters of each other's businesses and I wouldn't hesitate to refer my clients to these people or support others in my industry. I believe in the law of attraction and that help always comes back to you at some point in your life.

Confidence is built upon self-belief, knowledge and expertise.

So, be confident and don't underestimate yourself.

Conclusion

Money and business management is a complex beast. It is inevitable that you will make mistakes. However, through experience I've come to realise that if you surround yourselves with the right people, with the right mindset and the right skills and are not afraid to be challenged (particularly by yourself) then you are likely to get much better outcomes and achieve your life goals.

Do not underestimate having a sense of direction, even if you don't know what you want, because it will keep you organised and help manage your expectations of life, both now and in the future.

But most of all be kind to yourself and trust your intuition!

Action points

1.   **Establish goals** – if you don't know where you are going, you'll end up some place else.

2.   **Understand your cashflow** – a useful exercise to work out what your income and expenditure needs are now and in the future.

3.   **Identify and address income and expenditure shortfalls** – establishes affordability, as well as any financial solutions which may need to be considered.

4.   **Review any existing financial products or policies** – existing plans may help to reduce your shortfall or could be updated so that they become more aligned to your future goals.

5.   **Insure your plan** – consider using protection plans, so that you can protect your wealth and maintain cashflow during periods of illness or injury, or on the death of you or a loved one.

6.   **Understand your business** – does your business really have a buyer and can it be sold, or do you need to consider an alternative method of investing for the future?

7.   **Control your expenses and optimise your income** – are you making the most out of your business, could you save money or optimise income?

8.   **Consider which platforms will be suited to showcase your expertise** – do people know who you are, are you showcasing your talents and building a rapport with your ideal client?

9.   **Collaborating with the competition can be a win/win** – borrowing each other's audience can give you both more exposure.

10.   **Does your money mindset help or hinder your progress** – you can do all of the above but false narratives and unhealthy mindsets can keep you locked in a place of self-sabotage.

ZOË BRINN

Zoë Brinn is a conscious leadership consultant and systems strategist for small businesses. Zoë helps leaders who are socially, economically and environmentally conscious to develop their sense, and make sense, of the world.

The results of leaders working with Zoë include: gained time, improved productivity, and a positive culture within their business. Zoë's services consist of done-for-you system builds, leadership consultancy, and a hybrid of both. She also owns The Conscious Leaders' Club and speaks at events to further plant the seed of consciousness within leadership.

Zoë's background and qualifications are in senior leadership in education and English teaching. Although she now works primarily with small businesses, she is an examiner for English and a governor of a secondary school.

Find out more about Zoe at www.linktr.ee/zoebrinn

Leading With Meaning: How Conscious Leaders Inspire Purposeful Change

I used to visit four main places: my office, my classroom, my kitchen and my bed. How we kept our relationship going, I don't know! My then boyfriend, now husband, is THE most patient and loving man on earth. Now, before you start thinking this will be a tale of my time on the brink followed by my rise to fortune, I can tell you, it will be neither.

I have suffered and I have risen and, of course, my story is here, but I'd rather focus on what led me to do what I do, rather than dwell on the details of that. I'd like to tell you why you need to be (and how to be) much more aware in your business. I don't believe in 'head down' and get on with it anymore. I think we need to be not just looking forward but one step ahead and be conscious in our decisions around people and the planet – all the time looking for better ways to lead.

I'm a Welsh woman who was brought up in North London, initially by a strict mother and alcoholic father. I must state here that we were brought up well, my parents did what they thought of as their absolute best for us morally and financially, but we were not 'well off'. I was labelled as 'naughty' and 'disruptive' with what they would now call 'anger issues' and, of course, later in life I found out I had ADHD and dyscalculia. I couldn't

explain what was happening to me, as I didn't understand it, and the adults,

teachers and peers in my life grabbed at what they knew – I was a short,

redheaded, angry girl who could be scary at times. But that is not how I felt

inside, I just felt unheard and misunderstood, and tried harder and harder

to get that across to the people I cared about.

I carried this through my early adult years, never feeling like I'd achieved

anything, nor feeling proud of myself, nor worthy of attention. So, of

course, I had a few wild years and ended up in an abusive relationship.

After my son Sean was born, I freed myself and ran straight into the arms

of my knight in shining armour, and son number two, Rowan, came along.

We got married and lived happily ever after…

Ok, so that didn't happen! But a career in fitness, a degree, a post-grad,

another marriage and divorce, and a daughter (Ruby) later – I still wasn't

work-satisfied. At this point I was an assistant head of an English

department. I liked my job but didn't feel I was excelling. I knew I had

more inside me but felt it was stuck there. I know now, looking back, that I

nailed a lot of the things I did: I have awesome children because I am an

awesome mum; I was a great English teacher – the kids, parents and

teachers told me so. However, that underlying feeling of underachieving led

me to applying for a position as an assistant head of school and getting it.

Before commencing (but after signing the contract) the head resigned, so I started my position with the acting deputy being temporarily promoted to acting head and myself and another new assistant head having to take on not only deputy responsibilities but also those that the acting head hadn't got to grips with. And before you quite rightly say that the system "doesn't let that happen", I'm giving you a pantomime "oh yes it does!" Our whole leadership team, which wasn't big, shifted up.

'The system' was completely unconscious; we were overworked, overwhelmed and it was not just like we were hanging on for dear life, but also like we had people stamping on our fingers. I should add at this point, it was a small school for pupils with behavioural difficulties, and although it wasn't easy, the pupils weren't the problem, the system was. I mean, if we look back further, we are likely to find that the people in the local authority had too many schools to manage and probably not enough human resources to properly follow up on things, but this is the exact point at which I decided I needed to do something to change it.

Of course, I went about it all wrong at first – I used my summer to plan a wider range of lessons for English, Literature and Literacy across the school. I met with my counterpart leader 'Mary Maths' and between us we created a curriculum which specifically took into consideration every child's needs in the school. I also put together a whole school plan for digital competency, as well as collaborating on the whole school plan.

Without going into every aspect, I problem solved and data analysed the holy moly out of the school. I wasn't asked to do this much over the summer, but this was my solution to the difficulties I was experiencing. Because the problem was with the system. It still is. My problem, though, was that I thought it was up to me to fix it, by working harder, longer and becoming more obvious so that people would listen to me. After all, I had the answers, right?

So, there I am. I've seen that others are trying to cut corners to survive. I've seen that people are making it up as they go along, so that people don't realise they are time-deficient, and in the middle of it all? I still think I can fix it even though my own leaders are unaware that I, too, am burning out. Their leaders also haven't realised they need more support, and the more we all try, the more we can't 'see' each other. We are not conscious of the bigger picture and the people within it.

I last a week into the term. I'm not a crier, but I burst into tears in the middle of the corridor and can't stop. I literally can't stop the water running out of my eyes – I tried. Even when I wasn't upset anymore, it still keeps happening. Someone turned on my tap and my washer had gone. So, I broke – I really did. I broke because the system is broken. It didn't work for me as a child of that system and it didn't work for me as an adult working within that system. I had a nervous breakdown and even tried to problem solve that too – putting all the strategy in place to get myself out. It sounds cold, and sometimes it was, but I did get myself out. I gave up my whole career. I resigned, but that's what was needed to move forward, to get well. It was what I needed in order to realise how I could be the change maker I'd been striving to be.

At first, when I thought of what I might do next, if I'm honest, my pride and fear of returning to the system stopped me from getting back into teaching. The idea of being a leader in any other career wasn't appealing and so I thought I needed to do something easy, so that I could keep looking after myself and my family. No sooner had I had my official last day, the pandemic hit and we were in lockdown. My timing (if I'd have been able to control it) couldn't have been worse. Two weeks into what should have been the new, upgraded, business-owning version of Zoë, I found myself without a stable job, without furlough, without financial help (as my business was so new) and without a focus on anything other than keeping myself afloat.

My family were, and still are, my biggest inspiration; seeing them adapt to this ever-changing world made me realise that I needed to find something that fit my quirks. Even though five out of six of us were working from home, and I was worried that I'd not bring enough money in to support us, they were more concerned about my happiness in my job. My husband, Piet, whose superpower is mindfulness, helped me work out what I could do by just asking me. *Me*. He asked *me*.

He actually told me it was 'my turn', and that although I'd decided early in our relationship that I would make decisions around me, I had continued to serve everyone else. So, to work out how I'd create change whilst still being 'me', I asked myself, what did my ADHD allow me do really well? I needed something that let me be 'Velma' – super-focused and regularly geeky – but also let me be 'Sonic the Hedgehog' – ten-to-the-dozen multi-tasking and jumping from task to task – when I needed to be. I also wondered, what I could do to help people understand that 'I don't process numbers well' without it making me feel like a failure? I mean, I'd hid it in every career I'd had so far, but I needed to be wearing that t-shirt now.

And the answer came from my past, all that I couldn't quite make fit before now seemed like a blueprint for my future: I need to be active, I need a variety of tasks, I need to analyse, I need to problem solve and I need to lead. So, I just started. If you are ever wondering what to do next or how to do something – just start. You'll get all the questions and answers from trying.

I love developing people, seeing them reach their goals, and I also love the earth, nature and connection. At first, I just helped people out, but there was still something missing; I hadn't used what had happened to me to create the change I really wanted to. I wanted to change the face of leadership (big, eh?). I wanted to make sure leaders did more than just check in on their team. I wanted to create a culture where people came first, and business thrived because of it. I wanted to stop people from breaking, reduce their stress, help them to exercise resilience and enjoy good mental health so society becomes stronger and the workforce becomes well.

I decided to start a group called 'Conscious Leaders'. Admittedly, now I realise that not everyone saw this as I did – I had some rather scary people talking about how the matrix is real (now I'm not talking about conspiracy theory – which I do sometimes have a penchant for – I mean those who believe we are living in an actual alternative reality). I also had all the 'woo' appear, and although I feel energy and believe in the earth giving us what we need, this was more 'celestial', again, not what I had meant by 'conscious'.

My idea of conscious leadership (and there are lots of us about, I don't believe I invented it) is being fully aware of how our actions, whatever they may be, affect business, society and the planet. These actions within business take the form of language, hiring, managing human resources, productivity, processes, systems, the way we portray ourselves and ecologically positive decisions.

If we are consciously aware of our actions, we can make the workplace much more efficient and productive. Creating this positive culture in turn affects society as a whole, the environment and our own businesses. This is my big difference. If I can help people grow small businesses in a way that looks after these things, we will have a better world. I know that sounds straight forward, I'm not talking about us just 'doing our bit' or taking our eye off other aspects like selling, marketing etc. I'm talking about each of us having the awareness and knowledge in finding, training and retaining people who connect to our mission and values – those whose own actions are led by our mission so that our working relationships are solid. This makes for a happier, more secure workforce and growth for us all.

Conscious leading can make our business models more sustainable. I can't stress how important this is for any business that wants to survive. There has been enough 'using' of people over the years, it's creating a social deficit, people's mental health has suffered and it's time we looked after our employees, freelancers and clients. Otherwise we are in danger of being the leader that people don't want to work for, we are in danger of having high staff turnover, we are also then in danger of not meeting our clients' needs; we could become preoccupied with staff issues, or have new staff who are not yet at the skill level to look after those clients. You get the picture, and the bottom line is, if we can make other people's experiences of us and our business positive, why wouldn't we?

I now work with business founders to put the people, teams, systems and processes in place so people feel secure, businesses gain time and the planet thrives – you can come and find me for help with all that, but in this chapter I want to tell you some things you can easily do so you too can make a difference to people's working lives whilst also growing your business.

Firstly, sometimes people don't understand that people are not things. I know this sounds extreme but it's more easily done than people realise. People are not here to be used, no matter what your (or their) role in the workplace. A really easy way to make sure people feel valued within your team is to speak to them with respect, and use language that keeps them motivated and safe. Your team members are mothers, fathers, children, grandparents – think about how you'd like your family members spoken to. And I'm not just talking about a 'please' and 'thank you'. Greet them, make them visible, be careful that your language doesn't make them feel they are under an invisible pressure; it will go a long way to building a relationship with them. That's exactly what our aim should be: to build relationships with our clients, team members, staff and freelancers which will ultimately lead to a happier, more fulfilled, secure and sustainable business.

Another way to make sure people don't feel used is to create a consistent process around human resources. If you see some of your team as less valuable, they will too. If you have a six-month review for your staff, make sure it's for all of them, whether they're a full-time, employed business manager or a part-time freelance administrator. They will become team players if you treat them as a team, so don't exclude any of them. Make sure they all have access to the same benefits, and they all have a contract, with copies of policies and access to support, this will help them feel secure in their role and you are more likely to retain them.

Being aware of the people within your business goes much deeper than manners and processes, and I'll tell you why.

Let's look at a specific scenario… A freelance social media designer is on your team. Let's call them Bob. They are not working when you have your weekly meetings and do not have an email address connected to your business. They also don't really tell you much in conversation, and you hired them because your friend (who specialises in coaching people in a rare martial art) said they were good. But it's ok, they do a good job, don't cost much money and you're happy with them.

You might be thinking, well, I got lucky and we're ticking along, and you might be right. However, look at some alternatives. What if you moved the meeting so they could attend? Would this help them to make the work they produce more accurate? What if you set them up an email? Would this make them feel part of the team and be able to reach out to others more easily? What if you had conversations around Bob's interests and got to know them? Would this make them feel able to initiate new ideas? Could they be more valuable to your business because you placed more value on them? What if you searched for your next person deliberately? Consciously? Would you find someone who already has similar values, interests and ideas to you? I'm sure if someone asked you if you wanted a conscientious team player who brought innovation and enthusiasm to your business, you'd be more likely to hire them than 'good job Bob'! So either change things for

Bob or find the right person first time.

These benefits are simply put as: if you are aware of your actions around everyone in your team, you will create safety, a positive culture and your business will become more productive. If you put your people before your profit, you will make more revenue and make society a better place to work in. You see, my purpose is to create change by helping business founders to create change within their team culture.

Although I can't cover everything (I'd love to cover inclusion, diversity, delegation, bonuses, retention, sustainability etc. but I don't have enough space here) I must talk about developing people. One of the best ways to keep your business growing is to grow the people within it, and I don't mean in a controlling way. The best thing about working with small businesses is that they have so much (sometimes infinite) room to grow, and so developing businesses is one of the most exciting things I do.

The number one rule of developing others is this: 'ask them'. Ask them regularly. Ask them at interview and at every benchmark or pin-point they get to: What do you love to do, and how can I help you get that? Then, help them get there. The process of doing this over time will be invaluable in both yours and their development. You will see their successes, and support them when they are not quite there yet – you will lead! You will change and create change by adapting to both your business needs and the needs of that individual. Create leaders, not carbon copies of yourself, but genuine leaders with their own aspirations and goals. By putting in place development strategies that work for them as individuals, you will create a much richer, more fulfilling role for them. They, in turn, will become more of a specific part of your business and more valuable, not just through new skills they pick up but also through the deep connection they feel to your mission and to you as a leader.

If you are fearful of developing them 'out of your business', don't be. There are three things that could happen because of your dedication to, or lack of, developing them:

1. They leave because they feel their new skills can get them something more.

2. They leave because they are not being fulfilled or stretched in their role.

3. They stay because they can use their newer skills specifically in your business and they love that you are stretching them.

Of course, number three is the answer you want, but number two would be down to you (sorry to be blunt but that's your fault) and as for number one, if not due to unhappiness in their role, if your business can't give them their next opportunity then you've done some great work to build our future workforce. And if they do move on for whatever reason, you will have the experience and the processes in place to find and onboard your next successful team member.

Rather than me banging on again about how 'the system' doesn't work anymore (I'll let you decide whether it ever did), it might be worth looking at what we can do now in the current economic climate. Actual climate change is too big a discussion for this space, but I'd like to just touch on society and the changes we've seen recently, and how we need to consciously adapt to them.

So, if the school system, working environment, government, NHS and so on, are showing cracks, big cracks — why aren't we, as smaller businesses, changing quicker to suit the needs of the future? We are already seeing a few shifts in pattern: there are more home-educated children than ever before, there are fewer people entering skilled professions such as nursing, there are more small businesses, entrepreneurs and self-employed youngsters, and soon there will be a bigger part of the workforce who will be entering it without formal qualifications. Although, that doesn't mean that they won't have the drive, passion and unmeasurable skills to benefit our growing small businesses. In addition, there will be a further need for understanding around diversity as more neurodiverse, non-binary, multi-cultural, isolated (this list is way too long to include everyone) humans will bring their skills and experiences into the lives and businesses of those who may not have considered such a diverse range of people before. How can we be anything *but* conscious leaders?

Our small businesses can make a difference to people's lives, we need to be the next-generation leaders, not wait for the actual next generation. And I'm not talking about token policies or short-lived initiatives. We need real change. You need to ensure that you not only create the policy but that you live the policy, whilst also implementing and ensuring that others in your business do the same. You decide the culture of your team and business, and you drive it. Considering the people, both clients and team, and their needs is essential not just to your business growth but to the survival of it.

If you want to set yourself a task around this, try this: write down your core culture values. You may already have an idea of, or clearly defined, business values, your mission (the purpose) and business vision. If not, you'll need those as well.

Then use these to create your core culture values. You can do this as an over-arching statement or a bullet point list of three things that the culture will both stand for and by or, as a more detailed list of rule-type actions. You will need to include how you expect your team to run/behave when communicating with you, each other and clients. An even better idea is to get your team involved in this task so that you have a really rounded set of agreed criteria for a positive culture.

An example of this is 'We stand for respect, communication and transparency' or 'Integrity is at the heart of our inclusive team'. When you have done that and refined it, roll it out to your team. Display it in your office and where your team hangs out. Add it to team documents, and, most importantly, keep your team accountable to it. By creating change for the future within our businesses, we will create not only sustainable businesses, but a sustainable society.

Now you may have some questions and concerns around my suggestions so far. I expect that 'I'm already so busy, how am I supposed to do this too' or something to that effect might be one. Aside from my actual services being the solution to this, I want you to ask yourself: "How much time do I waste on tasks that can be outsourced?", "How much time do I waste on dealing with team problems due to not consciously hiring?", "How efficient are my processes, not just for my clients but also for my team?". You can gain time by leading; being the CEO, director or founder of your business is less about 'running' your business and more about leading it – creating the space for your team to work within it.

Consciously considering people and the planet whilst leading our business might mean we have to change, but change is good, and with the right processes to support this, we will see our small businesses growing, thriving and creating the time we need to move to our next stage. We, as small businesses, can collectively make more of a difference than any one corporation, and we should.

WORK WITH NICOLA

I help amazing people like you to create connections, grow your business and learn new skills, so you can live the life you deserve - by design!

If you are ready to take action and work on growing your business, I would love to help support you.

You can work with me 1-1, through my exclusive Masterminds or start initially by becoming a valuable member of Peakes Private Members Club.

To find out which would be the best route for you please register your interest below, and I will personally be in touch.

WORK WITH NICOLA

CONNECT WITH NICOLA

Printed in Great Britain
by Amazon

22253347R00108